01/02

WITHDRAWN

Mackay 12-02

DANTE

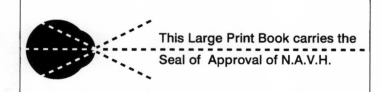

This Large Print Book carries the
Seal of Approval of N.A.V.H.

R. W. B. Lewis

DANTE

Thorndike Press • Waterville, Maine

VH
E
DANTE
.LE
2001

Copyright © R. W. B. Lewis, 2001

Grateful acknowledgment is made for permission to reprint excerpts from *Vita Nuova* by Dante Alighieri, Italian text with facing English translation by Dino S. Cervigni and Edward Vacta. Copyright © 1995 by University of Notre Dame Press. Used by permission of University of Notre Dame Press.

Map illustration by Peter W. Johnson

All rights reserved.

Published in 2001 by arrangement with
Viking Penguin, a member of Penguin Putnam Inc.

Thorndike Press Large Print Biography Series.

The tree indicium is a trademark of Thorndike Press.

The text of this Large Print edition is unabridged.
Other aspects of the book may vary from the original edition.

Set in 16 pt. Plantin by Al Chase.

Printed in the United States on permanent paper.

Library of Congress Cataloging-in-Publication Data

Lewis, R. W. B. (Richard Warrington Baldwin)
    Dante / R. W. B. Lewis.
      p. cm.
    Includes bibliographical references.
     ISBN 0-7862-3755-4 (lg. print : hc : alk. paper)
     1. Dante Alighieri, 1265–1321. 2. Authors, Italian — To
1500 — Biography. I. Title.
PQ4339 .L48 2001
851'.1—dc21
  [B]   2001053453

For Fausto, Rita, and Francesca Meiners
with gratitude and love

Special Sources

1. Cover Portrait of Dante

The painting shows Dante during his final years, in exile in Ravenna, 1319–1321. It was done, probably in the early 1860s, by Domenico Petarlini (sometimes spelled "Peterlin"), who was born in 1822 in Bagnolo di Longo in northeastern Italy and who studied and composed in Venice, Rome, Torino, and Florence before settling in Vicenza in 1865. He died in Vicenza in 1898. The influence upon him of European Romantic art seems evident in the pervasive sadness of the poet's figure and the inwardness of expression.

Petarlini was drawn especially to biblical and historical subjects. One of his better known paintings is a portrait of Savonarola, now in Berlin's Gemaldegalerie. Our portrait belongs to the Galleria d'Arte Moderna in Palazzo Pitti, Florence.

2. Map of Dante's Italy

The map was prepared by Peter W. Johnson, design director of RIS, a section of Yale University. From the outset, Peter Johnson showed himself zestful and courteous as well as highly skilled. In addition, he put us in touch with his son Benjamin, who was in Florence at the time, studying at the British Institute. Thereafter, Benjamin Johnson did invaluable research for us, making his way through the Florentine bureaucracy with admirable adroitness. All this comprises one of the most enjoyable episodes in the entire enterprise, and I am grateful beyond measure.

Contents

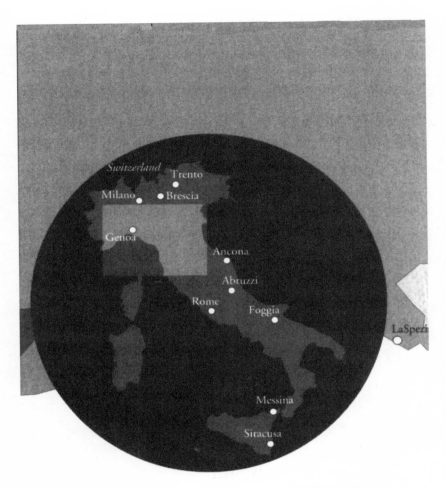

Switzerland Trento
Milano Brescia
Genoa
Ancona
Abruzzi
Rome Foggia
LaSpezi
Messina
Siracusa

Ligurian Sea

Sardinia

DANTE'S ITALY

Verona

Venice

Adriatic Sea

Bologna

Ravenna

Forlì

Rimini

Pistoia

Prato

Monte Falterona

Lucca

Fiésole

Pagnolle

Pisa

Arno

Florence

Campaldino

Caprona

Empoli

Arno

Siena

Arezzo

Tuscany

Perugia

one

Dante the Florentine

As you walk across the Ponte Vecchio in Florence today, you come upon a plaque bearing a passage from Dante's *Divine Comedy*. The lines are spoken by Dante's ancestor Cacciaguida, whom the poet encounters in one of the higher spheres of heaven, among the warrior saints. They reflect grimly on an event that took place on that very spot in 1216, almost fifty years before Dante's birth, and plunged the city into decades of turmoil. The event was the murder of Buondelmonte dei Buondelmonti, a feckless nobleman who had abruptly abandoned his betrothed, a maiden of the Amidei clan, for the richer and more beautiful daughter of the clever Madonna Donati. The Amidei were joined in vengeful outrage by their Uberti relatives; a group of them lay in wait for Buondelmonte on Easter morning, when he rode across the bridge on his white palfrey, himself suitably clad in gleaming white, and cut him to pieces.

This, Cacciaguida says, was the city's last

day of peace, and he thought it fitting that the assassination should be carried out near an ancient statue thought to be of Mars, the god of war. For civil warfare immediately ensued, in a ferocious battle for power between competing groups of Florentine families.

Dante was the supreme poet-historian of Florence, its most passionate observer, its most bitter and frustrated product. Scattered around the contemporary city are thirty other plaques with passages from the *Comedy*, evoking a range of places Dante had known and moments and persons he had known or heard about in his thirty-five years of Florentine life: the Arno and Ponte Vecchio; the venerable Baptistery (*mio bel San Giovanni*, Dante called it); Via del Corso, a main thoroughfare in Dante's neighborhood, with its cluster of rich and potent families; the church of San Miniato, perched high above the river on its south side; Brunetto Latini, the great humanist and Dante's tutor in classical literature; Farinata, the most valiant among the Florentine Ghibellines; and, of course, Dante's mythically beloved Beatrice. She is captured verbally in a passage near the end of the *Purgatorio*: a visionary presence who will escort Dante through the Christian

14

heavens, here garbed in a green mantle that seems to glow like a living flame, wearing a snow-white veil crowned with olive. The plaque offering this image is attached to No. 4 Via del Corso, on the palazzo that once belonged to Beatrice's father, Folco Portinari.

Dante associated himself with his native city to a degree almost incomprehensible in modern times. Florence was not merely his birthplace; it was the very context of his being. He was Dante Alighieri, a distinct individual with a classic profile and a sometimes tempestuous disposition. He had intimate friends, like his sportive neighbor Forese Donati; literary colleagues, like the older poet Guido Cavalcanti; and deadly enemies, like Forese's brother Corso. He was the dedicated lover, from a distance, of Beatrice Portinari, until her death at an early age in 1290, and a few years later he composed in her memory his first major work, the *Vita Nuova*, the story in prose and poetry of his devotion to her from the age of nine. In the course of time, Dante became a married man (his wife was another and more sedate member of the Donati clan), with three children. But he was an ardent personality, and more than once, in pursuit of other Florentine maidens, he lost the straight way, to borrow his phrase at the opening of the *Inferno*. Even in his lifetime, as the first two canticles of the *Divine Comedy* began to circulate (around 1315), he was recognized as the greatest Italian poet, the *sommo poeta*, of his age. But he was first and last a Florentine, and indeed, on one level, his masterwork, the *Comedy*, is an expression of his passionate feelings about Florence, his rage against the conspirators who had driven him out, his longing to return.

His entire life was entangled with the history of Florence, and that history in turn was in part the offspring of the old European struggle between the so-called Guelphs and the so-called Ghibellines. The two names are of German extraction — Welf and Weiblingen, respectively — and originally, in the twelfth century, referred to two combative noble German houses. As the controversy expanded in the early thirteenth century, the Ghibellines became the party supporting the claims of the Holy Roman emperor to absolute authority in Europe, and the Guelphs, the party backing the papacy in its rival claim. Guelphs and Ghibellines were next seen fighting it out within cities like Florence and Bologna; but by this time the two names referred not to the larger controversy but to warring local factions. In Florence, the Buondelmontes belonged to the Guelph party, and the Amidei and Uberti to the Ghibellines.

Within Tuscany, the Guelph/Ghibelline fracas reached two climaxes in the half century after 1215. (There were lesser upheavals along the way; the Ghibellines, for example, battering down thirty-six Guelph towers in Florence in 1248, and the Guelphs, replying in kind two years later, filling the streets with the rubble of smashed Ghibelline domiciles.) In 1260, at Montaperti, a village on the Arbia, near Siena, the Ghibelline hordes won a decisive victory. The leading Guelph families were banished and the city very nearly came to an end. The Ghibelline commanders, meeting at Empoli, west of Florence, voted to raze Florence to the ground. Only Farinata degli Uberti stood out against them, declaring himself to be a Florentine first and a Ghibelline second, and vowing that he would defend his native city with his own sword. The Ghibellines thereupon took the lesser course of knocking down 103 palaces, 580 houses, and 85 towers.

When the Guelphs regained control of the city in 1266, they expressed their gratitude to Farinata by destroying every building belonging to the Uberti clan, in what is now Piazza della Signoria, decreeing as well that no building should ever again be erected in that accursed space. (This is why Palazzo Vecchio, begun in the 1290s, is not in the center of the piazza, as one might expect, but squeezed over to one side.) Dante comes upon Farinata in the sixth circle of the *Inferno*, reserved for heretics, and hears the Ghibelline chieftain, motionless within his fiery tomb, asking about the harsh reprisals against his family. It was, Dante tells him,

> the havoc and the great slaughter
> that dyed the Arbia red

that had so roused the Florentine Guelph enmity. But in all of that, Farinata says, "I was not alone" —

> Yet I was alone when everyone else
> voted to destroy Florence,
> I alone with open face defended her.

In 1266, in any case, the Guelphs, under the leadership of Charles of Anjou (summoned to Italy by the crafty Pope Clement IV), utterly routed the Ghibelline forces at Benevento, northeast of Naples. The

Ghibelline imperialists had at their head Manfredi, an illegitimate son of the Emperor Frederick II and a man Dante rather admired, placing him in Purgatory, among the excommunicated, with a chance yet for salvation — "while hope still blossoms," in Manfredi's wistful saying. But for Dante's family and their friends, the victory at Benevento was the restoration of their lives and the making of their city. All the Guelph exiles returned; the Ghibellines never again occupied any corner of Florence, though they posed intermittent threats, as will be seen, in other parts of Tuscany.

Dante was one year old in 1266, and he grew up in a city that was at last fully realizing itself. It had been moving fitfully toward that goal for a good many years, in a series of developments that led both to prosperity and to a gathering self-image: a feeling for the primacy of the civic and the public over the private and the factional, combined with a sense of the larger importance of the merchant class as against the nobility. The Florentine merchants began to form themselves into guilds (or *Arti*) as early as 1206, when the Bankers' Guild was founded. There followed the Wool Guild of 1212, the Silk Guild on Por Santa Maria in 1218, and much later Apothecaries, Judges,

Notaries, and others, well into Dante's life-time. Eventually, there were seven "major" merchant guilds and fourteen "minor" (artisan) guilds: butchers, bakers, blacksmiths, leather workers, and the like.

The guilds were the source of stability and continuity in thirteenth-century Florence, a vital bureaucracy that held the society together and kept the economy expanding while Guelphs and Ghibellines came and went. The surging Florentine economy was based principally upon banking and international trade in luxury items, especially handsomely adorned leather goods. And it was a telling moment in the Florentine annals when, in 1252, the first gold florin was minted and almost instantly became the basic monetary measure in Europe. For it was engraved not, as had been customary, with the image of a pope or emperor but with the symbols of the city: on one side, San Giovanni, the patron saint of Florence; on the other side, the lily, the city's secular emblem.

Dante made a public gesture of allegiance in 1295 by entering the Guild of Apothecaries (by a bit of legal stretching, philosophers and men of letters could inscribe therein). Meanwhile, he could take pride in the ways the city was completing itself physically. By the time of his birth, four bridges spanned the Arno at strategic intervals, uniting the northern and southern sections and in particular making the hitherto disregarded section known as Oltrarno, beyond the Arno, a significant part of the urban whole. The bridge Buondelmonte rode across to his death in 1216 had then been the only passageway over the river. About five years later, a second bridge was erected a short distance downriver; it was given the name Ponte Nuovo, the New Bridge (it is now Ponte alla Carraia), and the preexisting one immediately — and for always — became known as Ponte Vecchio. A third crossing, upriver, was added in 1237 (Ponte alle Grazie today), and in the late 1250s a fourth bridge was built near the church of Santa Trinità, from which it took its name.

There remained one major, indeed enormous, architectural necessity: a new circuit of walls, to give Florence its distinct and lasting shape. This was an urgent human need as well. By the time Dante entered his teens, the population of Florence had grown to some eighty thousand, in Europe second only to Paris. But a great many of these *cittadini* lived outside the walls that had been built in 1172, when the population was less than thirty thousand. Such folks led a precarious existence, their homes routinely destroyed in pursuit of a scorched earth policy whenever Florence came under siege. Besides, to live outside the walls was not really to belong to the city at all. The city was by definition a walled entity, and a citizen — *cittadino* actually means one dwelling in the *città* — was one who resided inside the circuit.

Similarly, several of the city's most valued religious centers were, as of 1280, outside the walls: the convent and church of Santa Maria Novella, the Florentine home of the Dominicans, to the west; the then small church of Santa Croce, the Florentine home of the Franciscans (created in the late 1220s, soon after the death of Saint Francis), to the east; the convent of San Marco, to the north, and that of Santo Spirito, to the south. Dante in his early years studied betimes with the Dominicans and listened to the Franciscan friars preaching in the piazza outside Santa Croce, and to do so he had to make his way beyond the protective walls.

To bring these families and monuments into the city, the Florentine government known as the Secondo Popolo decreed in 1284 that a new and very much larger circuit of walls be constructed, and appointed the Tuscan-born architect Arnolfo di Cambio to design it. It was the successor not only to the 1172 circuit mentioned above but also to the ancient circuit of a century earlier, the *cerchia antica* later named for Cacciaguida and cited by him in *Paradiso* xv as source and symbol of a happier time:

Florence, within the ancient circling . . .
  abode
    in peace, sober and chaste.

Neither peace, sobriety, nor chastity was a feature of Dante's Florence; but the circuit of walls planned by Arnolfo di Cambio is among the great urban-architectural achievements of all time. It expanded the city in all directions; it not only brought the several churches and convents into the city but also, by a curvature of walls, related them to each other meaningfully, along fixed diagonal lines — the Dominican Santa Maria Novella to the northwest, the Franciscan Santa Croce to the southeast, and so on. The entire circuit was about five and a half miles in circular length; the walls stood forty-seven feet high and were seven feet thick, wide enough at the top for two soldiers to pass each other on patrol. There were fifteen massive gates, shouldering up to as much as 115 feet; every 370 feet there was a tower, seventy-three in all, with an average height of 75 feet. A wide road stretched along the walls within (portions of it form Florentine boulevards today) and another one outside, with a broad ditch circling both road and walls. The entire circuit was completed in 1333.

It was prodigious by communal intention, a great wall to enclose and to give shape and identity to a great city; and it remained so, intact and shape-giving, until its demolition in the late nineteenth century. As construction proceeded, Florentine citizens clustered about this segment or that, pointing with amazement and delight at the various gates and towers, arguing with one another about probable statistics. Dante, it may be assumed, was among these proud onlookers, watching, appraising, commenting. The experience, with others, led to the maturing Dante's conviction that Florence was the ideal city-state, which is to say, the ideal human habitat.

Drawing on the cultural legacy he had imbibed from Brunetto Latini, Dante came to believe that the city, the *città*, was the place where men and women could properly live and thrive — if the city were organized, ruled, and shaped in the Florentine manner of the 1280s. *Città,* in its richest meaning, was a term of utmost value for Dante. He could even imagine Paradise as a *città,* a heavenly city, and had obviously absorbed the Ciceronian idea, formulated in *De Natura Deorum* (with which Dante was reasonably familiar), that even the gods were "united in a sort of civic society," so that the entire universe could be thought of as a city of gods and men. And he could find the theme expressed in the opening lines of Virgil's *Aeneid,* the poem Dante most revered, where Virgil promises that his poem will tell of "a man who suffered much in war until he could found a city."

In his larger vision, Dante conceived of his own *mundus* as a constellation of well-formed city-states under the ideally balanced leadership of pope and emperor. But Florence was to be the exemplar among the urban centers. With this inspiring thought in mind, Dante served his city in military venture against the Tuscan Ghibellines in the 1280s and took part in civic affairs from about 1295 onward. In 1300 he served a term in the city government as one of the six priors, collectively known as the Signoria; and in its dealing, he became notable for putting the welfare of the commune above all other considerations.

It was another fateful period in Florentine history. The Florentine temper, then as later, was combative; and the Guelphs, so long the city's leaders, fell to quarreling vociferously with each other. In the fall of 1301, actual war broke out between them: between the White Guelphs, now so labeled, represented by Vieri de' Cerchi and oriented toward the merchant class; and the Black Guelphs, led by Corso Donati and favoring the nobility. Dante happened to be in Rome when hostilities began. He was in Siena, on his journey north, in March 1302, when the Black Guelphs summoned him to appear to answer criminal charges. When he failed to show, he was convicted of heinous and wholly trumped-up crimes and condemned to death. Dante never set foot in Florence again.

During his nineteen years of exile, and despite problems of sheer survival in the early period (he was reasonably comfortable later, in Verona and then in Ravenna), Dante became the complete creative writer. He was prolific almost beyond reckoning. In 1304 there came the *De Vulgari Eloquentia*, a tract on the superiority of the vernacular over Latin for the writing of poetry. Not long after came the *Convivio*, or "Banquet": a celebration of the mode of long lyric poem called a *canzone* (song), with Dante offering a number of his own canzones for analysis. Some time after 1308, Dante composed the *De Monarchia*, another Latin treatise, addressing the ideal relation of empire and papacy, inspired by the appearance of Henry of Luxembourg as the potential pacifier and uniter of Italy. But prior to that, Dante had launched upon his major enterprise, the three-part poem he simply called the *Commedia*, the term for him referring to a work that begins in misery and ends in happiness: from the souls in torment in the Inferno to the souls in blessedness in Paradise. But throughout, it is the voice of Dante the exiled Florentine that we hear.

The note is struck in the *De Vulgari Eloquentia*: "Of all who in this world are deserving of compassion, the most to be pitied are those who, languishing in exile, never see their country again, save in dreams." The *Commedia*, to which the adjective *Divina* was affixed two centuries afterward, is, all things considered, the greatest single poem ever written; and in one perspective, as has been said, it is autobiographical: the journey of a man to find himself and make himself after having been cruelly mistreated in his homeland. It is also a rhythmic exploration of the entire cultural world Dante had inherited: classical, pre-Christian, Christian, medieval, Tuscan, and emphatically Florentine. And it is the long poetic tribute to Beatrice Portinari which Dante promised, at the end of the *Vita Nuova*.

While completing the *Commedia* in Ravenna, in 1321, in a passage at the start of *Paradiso* xxv, Dante voiced his increasingly dreamlike hope of a return to his city:

> Should it ever come to pass that the sacred poem
>> To which heaven and earth have set their hand
>> So that it has made me lean through many a year,
> Should overcome the cruelty that shuts me out
>> From the fair sheepfold where I used to sleep,
>> A lamb, foe to the wolves who war upon it
> With a changed voice now, and with changed fleece,
>> I will return a poet, and at the font
>> Of my baptism I will take the laurel crown.

By 1321, the first two parts of the *Comedy* had been transcribed and sent in circulation

28

for some years, and Dante was being acclaimed through much of Tuscany as its greatest poet. But the Florentine authorities did not soften toward him, and the imagined ceremony of coronation at the baptismal font in San Giovanni never took place. Dante died on September 14, 1321, in Ravenna, and was buried there.

The first sign of official acceptance did not come until 1373, when the Signoria granted a petition, urged on it by a number of citizens, to permit Giovanni Boccaccio to offer a series of lectures on Dante's life and works. Boccaccio was the greatest and most influential admirer of Dante in his generation. The *Decameron*, like Boccaccio's other writings, is thick with allusions to stories and passages in the *Comedy*; Boccaccio also transcribed and composed a commentary on the poem. In the early 1350s, he compiled the first biography of Dante; it remains a unique and indispensable source. Boccaccio was Tuscan-born, in 1313, and in his early years he could listen to tales and legends about the still living Dante Alighieri. In later decades — Boccaccio spent a considerable period in Naples but returned to Florence around 1340 — he made a point of consulting people who had known Dante, including literary associates and followers. After 1345, Boccaccio lodged in the home of Lippa de' Mardoli, the second cousin of Beatrice Portinari, who could tell Boccaccio a great deal about Dante's youthful passion.

Boccaccio thus addressed his cultivated and attentive audience with an easy authority. The lectures began in late October 1373, and after an introduction at once reverential and spirited, in which Boccaccio spoke of Dante as "a very great poet" to whom all honor was due, he began to sketch out Dante's life, beginning with his ancestry. He told of the Eliseo clan, one member of which had come from Rome to Florence in earliest time and had settled there. Into this family, with the passage of years, Boccaccio continued, "there was born and there lived a knight by the name of Cacciaguida, in arms and in judgment excellent and brave." In his youth this knight's elders gave him as a bride "a maiden born of the Alighieri of Ferrara. . . ."

two

Neighborhood Presences: The Early Years

Cacciaguida was a Florentine figure of heroic legend, knighted by Emperor Conrad III, whom he followed on the Second Crusade to the Holy Land, where he was slain in battle in 1148 at age forty-two. He appears to Dante, in Paradise, like a star shooting along a glowing cross composed of the spirits of the courageous; and over three cantos (xv–xvii) he gives an eloquent discourse on the history and vicissitudes of the city of Florence, on the genealogy of the poet's family and the source of its name, and on Dante's future after 1300. Addressing Dante as his dear descendant, "my leaf," he informs him:

> . . . He from whom thy kindred has its name, and who a hundred years and more has circled round the Mount on the first terrace, was son to me, and thy grandfather's father.

The reference is to Cacciaguida's younger son, Alighiero, named, as was the custom, after the warrior's father-in-law and later known as Alighiero I. If he has been circling among the proud ones on Mount Purgatory for a hundred years, he has been dead (as of the imaginative encounter in 1300) since about 1200.

As to the sin for which Alighiero was doing penance, it was quite likely excessive pride of family. Cacciaguida's ancestors, bearing the name Eliseo, came from ancient Roman nobility; more than that, when Alighiero I married, around 1170, he entered the family of Bellincione Berti, another honored personality — simple-mannered but valiant, in Cacciaguida's image; and one that gave him as sister-in-law the maiden Gualdrada, *la buona Gualdrada* as Dante called her. She had demonstrated her goodness, or chastity, during a visit to Florence by Emperor Otto IV when, in the church of Santa Reparata (the precursor of the Duomo), her father, Berti, urged her to kiss the emperor, to which she replied that she would kiss no man except her husband. Much impressed, the emperor arranged a marriage between her and his henchman Guido Guerra of the vigorous and marauding family from the Casentino.

Berti's two other daughters married

scions of the Donati and the Adimari clans, already notable but not yet troublesome members of the Florentine scene. So Alighiero I, looking about him, could indeed locate a series of famous names among his kinfolk. Dante, perhaps thinking about his great-grandfather, seems to disdain such family vanity: *"O poca nostra nobiltà di sangue"* [how paltry is our pride of race] (*Par.* xvi); and yet he admits having yielded to the emotion.

Alighiero I named a younger son after his father-in-law. About this second Bellincione we know that he led a long life and that in the 1250s, during the Primo Popolo, the city's first quasi-popular government, he held a position of respect. His own younger son, Alighiero II, was the father of Dante Alighieri.

Dante was born in the latter part of May 1265. During his first months, he was known around the household as Durante, presumably after his maternal grandfather, who is thought to have been Durante degli Abati (the name appears later, at a crucial moment in the family story, as a guarantor of a big loan transacted by the younger Alighieris). Durante was shortened to Dante at the time of the infant's baptism in March 1266, along with all the other children born in Florence since the previous March, in the stately old Baptistery of San Giovanni, with its interior of mosaics and marble and its exterior of solid rustic stone.

Dante's father made a modest but adequate living from the rental of property, both within Florence and outside in the country, and from moneylending. Dante's friend and literary associate Forese Donati, in a somewhat spiteful letter in the 1280s, accused the elder Alighieri of the sin of usury. This was evidently quite untrue. In the *Inferno*, in the seventh circle, Dante comes upon the usurers, those who had charged exorbitant sums for loans of money. They are a bad lot, and they are huddled in burning sand, with flames licking about their heads. Dante peers intently into their tear-stained faces and makes a point of saying, "I knew not any of them." The fact that Alighiero II was not himself among the Guelphs banished from Florence when the Ghibellines took over in 1260 suggests clearly that he was not conspicuous for either his wealth or political activity.

Dante's mother was Bella (short for Gabriella) degli Abati, a family of considerable wealth and property, with houses in town and castles in the country. But it was a strongly Ghibelline family and fell into disfavor after one member, Bocca degli Abati, performed treacherously at the battle of Montaperti in 1260. Dante finds him in the ninth, and lowest, echelon of hell, encased in ice, along with other traitors to their own country. Dante kicks him in the face and pulls his hair, making the culprit yelp with pain and outrage.

Bella and Alighiero II had a younger child, a daughter, to whom Dante refers affectionately, as it seems, in the *Vita Nuova*, as the kind young woman, joined to him "by the closest blood-tie," who looked after him during a "sorrowful sickness." Then Bella died, in 1272, when Dante was seven years old. His father quickly remarried, to Lapa di Chiarissimo Cialuffi, almost totally unknown despite her ringing middle name. The couple had a son, Francesco — Dante would grow close to his stepbrother — and two daughters. But Alighiero II died in the early 1280s, and Dante, in his late teens, was suddenly the male head of the household. One cannot with any certainty measure the effect upon Dante of these parental losses. At several moments in the *Comedy* — with Virgil, with Brunetto Latini, with the poet Guido Guinizelli — Dante seems to be searching for another father, a spiritual and literary father, as it were. The image of a "true mother" is gradually absorbed by the figures in Paradise of Beatrice and the Virgin Mary.

The Alighieri houses were in the *sestiere* of San Piero Maggiore, a northern urban area spreading east from the ancient *mercato vecchio* (now the Piazza della Republica), essentially along Via del Corso, to the city gate for which the section was named. Florence had been divided into *quartieri* (quarters) at the time of the 1078 circuit of walls; but with the construction of the much larger circuit, beginning in 1172, the commune voted to carve the city into sixths, *sestieri*, or, as sometimes written, *sesti*.

The *sestiere* San Piero Maggiore was age-old family territory. Cacciaguida's ancestors were born close by, the crusader says, and identified the spot more precisely:

> where he who runs in your annual race
> first enters the last *sesto*.

The race was held on June 13, the feast of San Giovanni, patron saint of Florence; and it consisted in fact of a dozen well-trained riderless horses sweeping across the city, west to east, guided by the lines of cheering Florentines and entering the last *sestiere* at the start of Via del Corso, itself named for the race.

Religion in all its aspects was, for Dante as for many (not all) Florentines, close to the center of life, and he could locate himself first of all in relation to the churches visible from the Alighieri windows. The little church of San Martino del Vescovo (St. Martin, Bishop of Tours is the figure invoked), a few steps away, was where the family went for daily prayers and Sunday services. Across the way was the Badia, the Florentine abbey founded in the heart of town in 978, through a huge gift of land and houses by the Countess Willa, and by 1250 a rich complex of chapels, gardens, libraries and shops. From childhood onward, Dante could hear the Badia bells chiming the canonical hours and so organize his day.

The *sestiere* was a neighborhood with families and individuals of great and often terrible importance for thirteenth-century Florence and in the life of Dante Alighieri. Above the Alighieri houses were the backs of the spacious homes of the Donati family, of whom Forese Donati would become a good friend of the poet in his skittish way, and Forese's brother Corso would turn into Dante's and the city's worst enemy. A little farther to the north, opposite the Baptistery, were the eye-filling homes and towers of the Adimaris, an extremely wealthy and influential family, about whom Dante, via his ancestor, speaks in the *Paradiso* with carefully contrived poetic venom:

> The outrageous tribe that is a dragon
>   to those who flee, but a lamb to any
>   who show their teeth or their purses.

When Dante was on the run in 1302, one of the Adimaris pounced like a dragon on his confiscated property in revenge, it seems, for Dante's action as a prior two years before in sentencing a young Adimari most harshly for his lawless public behavior. And then, a short distance to the east, lay the massive holdings — palaces and piazzas, courtyards and gardens — of the Cerchis, a more recently arrived, enormously rich and, for many Florentines, an infuriatingly upstart clan, charged with family pride.

As the century waned, the San Piero Maggiore region became known as the *sesto degli scandali,* the scandalous sixth: and this because out of it came the ferocious civil war, the murderous attacks and counterattacks, that tore the city apart and led to the banishment of Dante and so many others. It was in its local origins a war between the next-door neighboring families of the Donatis and the Cerchis. Dante initially, though with little enthusiasm, sided with the White Guelphs and went into exile with them. But, as we will see, it was not long before he disassociated himself from both factions and, in the formula of his forebear, appointed himself a party of one — "a party of your self."

Finally, and literally within a stone's throw of Dante's home, were the solid houses built there by Folco Portinari, the father of Beatrice.

Dante's early years were not spent entirely within the walls of Florence. Fond allusions in his poetry to country scenes, to hills, woods, and streams, testify to his frequent sojourns in the Alighieri farmlands, north of town in the direction of Fiesole. Part of the family income came from the rental of these properties, and they needed to be overseen from time to time. The most cherished, for Dante, was Pagnolle, to the east, about eight miles above the present Pontassieve, amid the green mountains curving toward the Casentino, near the Sieve River as it courses downward to the Arno. Another favorite setting was Camerata, a more fashionable little area on the road that leads up from Porta al Pinti (created with the 1284 circuit) to Fiesole.

The first of May in Florence was the occasion for neighborhood gatherings to celebrate the full arrival of spring and the appearance of colorful Tuscan flowers. On May 1, 1274, Folco Portinari gave a party for the residents of San Piero Maggiore. The elder Alighieri was invited and, followed by nine-year-old Dante, made his way along the narrow passage from his home, past the little church of Santa Margherita, to the large-scale palazzo of the Portinaris on the Corso. Here, among the other young ones, Dante for the first time laid eyes on Portinari's daughter Beatrice. He was captivated on the spot, and remained so in fact and in visual and poetic memory all his life.

Folco Portinari was then a man in his prime and one of the most truly admired individuals in Florence, "a citizen of great distinction, and possessed of many talents" in Boccaccio's judgment, a man "in the highest degree good" in Dante's. Portinari would serve two terms in the Signoria, as a judicious member of the city government. But beyond that, he displayed a generosity of spirit rare indeed in a Florence so characterized by pugnacity and greed. He was tireless in his support of the sick and the needy, and even of stray animals. In 1285, after several years of planning, he began the construction of a hospital, on family lands just outside the walls, specifically for the poor. It opened in 1288 and was dedicated to Santa Maria with the name of Santa Maria Nuova. (It is today one of the city's leading hospitals, and the current Via Portinari angles up to it from the Corso.)

Monna Tessa, who had taken care of Beatrice as a child, was put in charge of the nursing, and she brought together a corps of oblates, religious women dedicated to the service of the sick, the first such nursing staff on record. The creation of Santa Maria Nuova was a truly memorable act in the epoch; and it is not surprising that, as Dante would write, Beatrice wept so bitterly upon the death of her father in 1289.

Portinari was married to Clia de' Caponsacchi, whose family had owned vast estates in Pagnolle, atop a hill overlooking the Alighieri farm. The Caponsacchis came to Florence in the twelfth century (Cacciaguida once more supplies the date) and built themselves houses near the *mercato vecchio,* in the San Piero Maggiore section. The Portinaris had ten children, among them five daughters, of whom Beatrice was the eldest.

In the *Vita Nuova*, the remarkable blend of reminiscence and poetic forays put together in the early 1290s, Dante tells of his first glimpse of Beatrice, she being at the start of her ninth year, as he calculates, and he near the end of his. "She appeared humbly and properly dressed," he remembers, "in a most noble color, crimson girded and adorned in the manner that befitted her so youthful age" — adorned, it may be supposed, with a wreath of flowers suitable for the occasion and for her youth. It was then that the boy's entire being yielded to the supreme power of Love, in the poet's later idiom.

Following Love's command, Dante sought out Beatrice "many times in my childhood"; sought her out in the walkways of the *sestiere* and even more in the little church of Santa Margherita, the parish church of the Portinaris, where Beatrice came to pray with her mother and Monna Tessa, almost every morning. Here Dante could sit not ten feet away and gaze at her in silent ardor. Gradually, he came to see in her "such noble and laudable bearing that of her could certainly be said those words of the poet Homer: 'She seemed no child of mortal man but of God.' "

With the passing of days, Dante's rudimentary education went forward, in a local school perhaps, and sometimes with a private tutor. He evidently read Priscian, the sixth-century Latin grammarian (he puts Priscian in Hell alongside Brunetto Latini and the other sodomites, but this may be in part a case of mistaken identity), as well as a book of moral instruction that he learned by rote, the fables of Aesop, and a treatise on polite behavior. The medieval Latin he was introduced to proved a hindrance rather than a help to the reading of Virgil, Cicero, and Boethius a decade afterward, under the guidance of Latini. But Dante absorbed everything — philosophy, theology, literature, history — and forgot nothing; and his visual imagination was being stirred constantly by wanderings in the interiors of the great churches of Florence and to the bridges and the distending vistas of river and hills that they afforded.

There seems to have been no question at any time of a formal engagement between Dante and Beatrice Portinari. Such matters were entirely the province of the parents, and the Alighieris and Portinaris had other plans. On February 9, 1277, one of the few dates in Dante's early life that can be established with precision, Dante was formally betrothed to Gemma Donati, the daughter of Manetto Donati. Dante was not yet twelve; Gemma was about ten. But it was a binding contract of marriage; breaking an engagement was a major offense in Florence, and, as we have seen in the case of Buondelmonte de' Buondelmonti, could lead to murderous revenge and civil violence. A ring was placed on Gemma's finger; and she brought to the ceremony a dowry described as twice the customary amount.

It was a large sum, but rather modest in view of the enormous wealth of the Donati family. It had made its name as early as 1065 by founding a hospital near the church of San Piero Maggiore (it was later transferred to the Vallombrosa hills). The Donatis were generous patrons of the parish churches of San Martino and Santa Margherita. Their lordly houses and towers dominated the Corso, and one of their houses shared a rear wall with the house in which Dante was born.

Sheer proximity of property and residence was most likely a prime reason for the betrothal. In addition to being next-door neighbors in Florence, the Donatis and Alighieris owned adjoining agricultural territory in Pagnolle; Dante and Gemma could have waved to each other many a time across the fields. And there was already a family relation of sorts: Manetto's grandfather Uberti, the founder of that branch of the clan, had married one of the daughters of Bellincione Berti and was thus a brother-in-law of Alighiero I, Dante's great-grandfather. (According to Cacciaguida, Uberti was much displeased that Berti then gave him one of the contemptible Adimaris as another brother-in-law.)

Manetto Donati was a kindly individual, ready to help out financially at later moments. His daughter Gemma was a serious, steady girl, so one gathers, nice-looking if not of such beauty as to make the pulse throb. Some eight years after the civil contract was signed in 1277, there would be a religious ceremony, and the young couple would take up their life together. Dante never once mentions his wife Gemma in any of his writing, nor are there any sly hints of domestic discontent. On the purely literary level, Gemma Donati may be said to have supplied Dante with an essential requirement in the troubadour tradition that he would soon be following poetically: a faithful wife to make it impossible for him to do anything vis-à-vis his loved one except to look at her with hopeless longing.

three

Love, Poetry, and War: The 1280s

Nine years after Dante first beheld Beatrice, and again on the first of May, in 1283, the young woman actually spoke to him. With two other ladies "of greater years," Dante says in the *Vita Nuova*, Beatrice was passing along the street; she looked up to where Dante was standing frozen to the spot. "In her ineffable courtesy . . . she greeted me, such that I then seemed to see all the terms of beatitude." Feeling thus wholly blessed, Dante went home and fell asleep. In his dream he saw the figure of Love, his lord and master, holding in his arms the lady who had just greeted him, "naked except that she seemed to me wrapped in a crimson cloth." In one hand Love held Dante's heart, which he gave to the lady to eat, after which he broke into bitter weeping and, with the lady in his arms, seemed to ascend to heaven.

When he had recovered himself, Dante wrote a sonnet about the dream-experience — he had already, he observes, had some self-taught practice in "the art of saying words in rhyme" — and sent copies of it around the city to the *fedeli d'Amore,* with whom Florence was packed: devotees of the lord of Love, who wrote poems to their master and recited them in little gatherings all over town.

The sonnet began:

A ciascun alma presa e gentil cuor
[To every captive soul and gentle heart]

It went on to invite his readers to give their own views on the event being described. Then Dante set forth his dream, from the appearance of Love to his departure, weeping, bearing the lady in his arms. To this missive there were many replies, with as many different readings of the vision. "Among the correspondents," Dante says, "was one whom I call first among my friends." This was Guido Cavalcanti, who sent along a sonnet beginning:

Vedeste, al mio parere, omne valore
[You saw, in my opinion, all worth]

Having seen the lord of Love, the sonnet implies, Dante had seen all that was best, all the moral and intellectual virtues bound into a single figure. It was a handsome tribute, coming from the individual who was regarded as the most brilliant Florentine poet writing in the "new style," and one of the city's most striking personalities.

Guido was the son of Cavalcante de' Cavalcanti, with whom Dante holds a faltering conversation down in the sixth circle of Hell (*Inf.*, x, 52–57). Cavalcanti, being punished as a heretic, rises up from his fiery tomb next to Farinata degli Uberti, the brave Ghibelline. It is a suitable place for him, since his son Guido had married the daughter of Farinata, in one of the several betrothals that aimed, without much effect, to lessen the tension between Guelph and Ghibelline families. Cavalcanti had been a rich and good-looking man, with a large house near the *mercato vecchio* in San Piero Maggiore. To Dante, he asks piteously about Guido, "Where is my son, and why is he not with you?" Dante hesitates to answer. The pilgrim knew, in 1300, that Guido had been exiled, partly through Dante's own act (as will be described); the poet, writing ten years later, knew that Guido would be back in Florence and dead of malaria before the year was out.

Guido Cavalcanti was about ten years older than Dante and, astutely recognizing the remarkable talent of the eighteen-year-old, became as it were an older brother, both poetically and personally, to Dante. Their friendship flourished through continuing exchanges and conversations. There came a moment when Dante addressed one of his most enchanting lyric poems to Guido and their fellow Tuscan poet Lapo Gianni, *"Guido i' vorrei che tu e Lapo ed io . . ."*

> Guido, I wish that Lapo, thou and I
> > Could be by spells convey'd, as it were now
> > Upon a barque, with all the winds that blow
> Across all seas at our good will to lie.

They would sail free of human cruelty and spite, the sonnet continues (in Dante Gabriel Rossetti's translation), and the wizard who had set them on their magic journey would see to it that their adored ones were present, and they would not "talk of anything but love."

Dante also speaks admiringly of Lapo Gianni in *De Vulgari Eloquentia*. Tuscans generally, he says there with unrepressed savagery, "are imbecilic in their language," and yet a few have attained excellence: "Guido, Lapo and another" — that is, himself — "all from Florence, and Cino da Pistoia." The last-named was another and younger poetic correspondent and a jurist in the making.

Dante's father died (in the early 1280s), close to the time when Dante's spirits were being kindled by Beatrice's courteous greetings and by the flurry of poetic composition and exchange that followed. Dante, now an orphan (with a stepmother), immediately took charge of his father's slim business affairs, as a first step selling the letters of credit the older man had held for outstanding loans. Dante was, for the moment, in funds.

But Dante quickly found another father, a figure of incalculably greater importance to him culturally, politically, and humanly than Alighiero II. This was Brunetto Latini, in many respects the key figure and certainly the representative man in the richly productive history of Florence from 1266, when the Guelph party took command after the victory at Benevento, until his death in 1294. This is the man whose "dear and kind paternal image" — so the poet tells him when they meet in the seventh circle of the *Inferno* — was fixed in his mind and his heart. Latini, in turn, addresses Dante in a kind of tender grief as "my son."

Latini, born around 1220, was already a citizen of renown when in 1260 he was sent on a political mission to King Alfonso of Castile. On his return journey, at Roncesvalles, he met a scholar from Bologna of whom he asked for news from home. The scholar told him of the massive Ghibelline victory at Montaperti, saying, as Latini would put it, that the Guelphs were driven from the city and that "the losses were great in imprisonments and death." Latini thereupon settled in France for six years, directing his energies to philosophy and literature. He composed the *Livres dou tresor*, a vast encyclopedic work written in French and long held in high esteem by French readers, and the *Tesoretto*, an allegorical excursion composed in Italian. He also completed a translation into Tuscan Italian of Cicero's rhetorical treatise *De Inventione* and a translation of Aristotle's *Ethics*. With these and other achievements, Brunetto Latini brought classical literature into the world of thirteenth-century Florence.

He was back in Florence within weeks of the Guelph victory in 1266, and from that moment on he was a leading voice in the city's politics and culture. He became senior advisor to the Guild of Judges and

Notaries in 1272, was for a period the chief notary in the city (the indispensable man in any important urban transaction), and served on several missions to foreign potentates.

For Dante and others in the literary community, Brunetto Latini was a true role model: the man of letters who was energetically active in public affairs and for the welfare of the city. He was a "great philosopher," in the sage judgment of Giovanni Villani, Florentine chronicler and friend of Dante; and he was the "fat-remover" (*disgrossatore*) from the bloated writings of the Florentine bureaucrats — a crucial role, then as always; and he taught them the arts of "speaking well and guiding and ruling the republic."

Latini played an important part in transforming Florence into something not very far from a republic. The immediate process began in 1279 with a visit to Florence by Cardinal Latino Malebranca, the learned and skillful nephew of Pope Nicholas III, the author of the grandly solemn hymn *Dies Irae*, and a severe moralist who chastised the Florentine women for their gaudy apparel. With the laudable aim of restoring peace in Florence, he urged the return of the Ghibelline exiles and even held large open-air meetings at which leading figures from both parties knelt on the ground and kissed one another on the mouth. Among the Guelph participants were Guido Cavalcanti; Dante's father-in-law, Manetto Donati; and Brunetto Latini.

The accord, such as it was, did not last very long. The Guelphs, settled in power, were proving no less vindictive and violent than the Ghibellines had been. But next, a number of enlightened citizens, Latini conspicuous among them, moved to create an urban authority quite independent of both warring factions. It would consist of selected representatives from the merchant class — that is, from the guilds of trade that, as mentioned, had been coming into prominence for some time. There were now twenty-one guilds across the city: major (bankers, wool makers, judges, and others), medium (bakers, shoemakers, and the like), and minor (hotel keepers, armor makers, and so on). Power was invested — this was the key feature — in three priors, elected for a period of three months, and during that period, the ruling authority, the Signoria, in Florence.

The three priors were housed in the tall rugged Tower of the Castagna so that, in the phrase of a contemporary observer, "they might be free from the threats of the *potenti*," the jealous nobles and men of wealth. The Torre was next to the Badia and directly across from the home of Dante Alighieri. The first priors entered the Tower in 1282. Brunetto Latini was one of the three in 1286.

The time would come in the mid-1290s when Dante would seek to fill the shoes of his departed master (who died in 1294). But in the 1280s, the influence of Latini showed mainly in the expansion of what might be called Dante's cultural horizon, as the younger writer began to read and absorb the works of Cicero, Boethius, and finally Virgil. Latini's aesthetic impact on Dante's poetry, meanwhile, was not very great; and Dante in these happy years was mainly occupied with his ongoing courtship of Beatrice Portinari and the poetry it engendered.

That courtship took several bizarre turns, if we accept Dante's account of the affair in the *Vita Nuova*, as, on balance, we probably can. One day, Dante records, Beatrice was seated in her usual pew in Santa Margherita, with Dante stationed nearby. Halfway between them was another "gentle lady of pleasing aspect" who kept staring at him; and Dante heard someone behind him remark that this second lady had obviously "devastated" the young man. Dante immediately played up, with the idea of using the "gentle lady" as a screen (*schermo*) for his true love. He made such a show of hiding his secret love for the screen-lady that everyone assumed that she was of course his beloved.

Dante even composed a few "little things in rhyme" for the screen-lady, though he holds back from quoting any of them. The romantic game went on for a goodly stretch, "some years and months" in Dante's phrase, and at one point he felt such a surge of good feeling toward the screen-lady that he resolved to speak her name openly in a poem, and did so, as he tells us, in a work that sang "the names of sixty of the most beautiful ladies in the city," those of Beatrice and the screen-lady buried in the inventory.

But there came a day when the screen-lady was obliged to leave Florence and "journey to a faraway city." Dante, worried that people would be suspicious if he did not make a show of grief, devised a rather prosaic sonnet, which began:

O you who along the way of Love
pass by, attend and see
if there be any grief as heavy as mine.

In the *Vita Nuova*, Dante does not hint at the fact that during this same time — in 1286 or thereabouts — he fulfilled his marriage contract with Gemma Donati, in the traditional religious ceremony in the Church of San Martino del Vescovo. They began their life together in the Alighieri house across the way. Their first child, Giovanni, was born apparently in 1287.

Looking back on his relationship with Brunetto Latini in these same years, Dante declares his gratitude in a teasingly ambiguous phrase during their exchange in the seventh circle of the *Inferno* (*Inf.*, xv, 82–87). "For in my memory is fixed and now goes to my heart," he says, bending down reverentially toward the older man —

> the dear and kind paternal image of you
> when in the world hour by hour
> you taught me how man makes himself eternal;
> and while I live, my tongue, I think
> should show what gratitude I have for it.

"How man makes himself eternal" — *come l'uom s'etterna*. The reference cannot be to immortality through great literary achievement — Latini's literary gifts were not of that highest kind — nor can it be a theological statement; Latini was in no way a religious counselor. Most likely, Dante is acknowledging the inspirational value of the *Tesoretto*, the long, incomplete, allegorical work that Latini put together during his exile years in France. It is the account of a journey through the next world in search of redemption. In the course of it, the pilgrim must make his way through a dark wood and ascend a mountain where he meets a guide, who begins to teach him the rudiments of astronomy. Here the poem breaks off, probably because Latini heard that the way was clear for him to return to Florence. The *Tesoretto* was thus in some important ways a model for the *Comedy*, a work enacting the search for eternal life. (Piero Bargellini has argued the point most persuasively, even when observing that the *Tesoretto* is literarily "insipid.") Dante the pilgrim foresees the moment when, in exile, the poet will compose a drama of redemption for which Latini's poem was the honored predecessor.

So the two of them pace along and talk together, Latini, naked, treading the burning plain that is his eternal agony, and Dante walking on a roadway just high enough to be out of reach of the flames. They have greeted each other in a warm and wondering manner. "What a marvel!" exclaims Latini, and "Are *you* here, Ser Brunetto?" cries Dante in return. The master foresees Dante driven out of Florence by his political enemies, whom he denounces with all of his old vigor as a people "avaricious, envious, and proud," descendants of that evil element, the Fiesolans, who were among the founders of the city. He also predicts a shining future for Dante the poet:

> If you follow your star
> you cannot fail to reach a glorious port,
> if I discern rightly, in the fair life.

The question remains why Dante placed his teacher and role model in Hell, among those guilty of violence against nature and, specifically, of sodomy. Homosexuality was, needless to say, an unredeemable sin in Dante's Catholic world; but there is no evidence anywhere, outside the *Comedy*, that Latini was homosexual. (For what it is worth, Latini was married and had several sons.) The matter has been endlessly argued by the commentators, with some slight indication that Dante's early readers themselves were astonished at the charge.

The literary consequence is certain: a nearly unbearable tension between Dante's love and admiration for Brunetto Latini, and the old man's humiliation and perpetual pain. The moral and religious laws of the universe may not be breached, Dante may seem to be saying, even by one as noble as Brunetto.

But another age-old poetic impulse may also be at work, the one that the critic and theorist Harold Bloom has named "the anxiety of influence," whereby a literary artist, as a mode of self-identification, discounts and denies the influence — even the importance — of a great predecessor. In American literary history, we have the example of Henry James belittling his unmistakable literary forebear Nathaniel Hawthorne. But as such language suggests, there is also somewhere in the downscaling treatment a shadow of the father-killing process.

Having completed his portrait of the old master, Dante, in his last glimpse of Brunetto, gives us one of the most stirring images in the entire *Comedy*. It derives from the annual footrace in Verona on the first Sunday in Lent, something Dante had seen more than once as an exile in the city: the naked contestants running across an open field, with the first prize being a bolt of green cloth:

Then he turned back, and he seemed
like one of those
        who run for the green cloth of
        Verona
        through the open fields; and of them
        he seemed
one who wins rather than one who loses.

On his trips out to the Alighieri farmlands in Pagnolle, Dante, it may well be
imagined, journeyed on horseback; a phase
of his education had been in the skills of
horsemanship, including those of caval-
ryman. As a member of a family of noble
ancestry, Dante was trained as a matter of
course in the knightly arts and could expect
to be called on for military service in time
of need.

Dante may have taken part in a foray of
November 1285, when he was still in his
twenty-first year. The Sienese had asked for
help from Florence in quelling an uprising
incited by the Ghibellines in Arezzo, and
Florence sent down a cavalry contingent. In
an elusive passage in the *Vita Nuova*, Dante
speaks of riding away from the city at about
this time on a journey that displeased him,
since it took him away from his beloved. He
might have been going forth to war or perhaps merely on a three-day hunting party.

Four years later, in any case, Dante was definitely in the forefront of the Florentine battle line when the Florentines met the Aretines head-on, at Campaldino in the Casentino Valley on June 11, 1289. The Ghibelline forces in Tuscany had been biding their time since their stinging defeat at Benevento in 1266. But in the later 1280s, they managed to seize control of Arezzo, just fifty miles southeast of Florence and up the course of the Arno River. The Guelph hegemony was clearly threatened.

It was decided, presumably by the priors of the moment, to send a force south to engage the Aretines, and by a sort of secret ballot the military commanders chose not to head due south along the river but to move eastward across the mountains to a convenient battle site. So it was that the Florentine cavalry, Dante among them, rode up over the Consuma Pass and down into the Casentino to the broad open field called Campaldino (*campo* of course means "field") directly below the hilltop fortress of Poppi, where the treacherous (to the Florentines) Guido Novello resided.

The Aretines marched up from the south; and the two forces drew opposite each other in battle array, on the morning of June 11, almost as though they were about to meet in a jousting tournament. The Florentines, with their allies from Siena, Lucca, Pistoia, and elsewhere, fielded about a thousand cavalrymen, flanked on both sides by ten thousand foot soldiers carrying big white shields. The supreme commander of the Florentine army was one Amerigo di Narbona, young, hardy, inexperienced. At the head of the cavalry was Dante's neighbor Vieri dei Cerchi. At the rear was a reserve force of cavalry, led by another neighbor, Corso Donati, who was then the podesta, or chief magistrate, of Pistoia. Amerigo had instructed Corso firmly not to stir unless given the order.

The Aretines, supported by allies from the north and east, numbered distinctly fewer than the Florentines. At their head was Buonconte da Montefeltro, a gallant Ghibelline warrior; the person actually giving orders was the Bishop of Arezzo, a belligerent personality but fatally myopic in both mind and eyesight. Staring over at the white shields of the Florentines, the bishop asked impatiently, "What are those white walls over there?" Buonconte would have preferred to hold back a little, to study the Florentine intentions, but the bishop called him a coward and a traitor and commanded the Aretines to charge.

They did so, and managed to break through the Florentine forward lines. But while the horsemen were prancing about in exultant disorder, Corso Donati, disobeying instructions, led his cavalry unit in a furious attack that dispersed the Aretines entirely and led to a total rout. Some seventeen hundred Aretines were killed, and three thousand were taken prisoner. But the Florentines were prevented from taking full advantage of their victory when a torrential storm descended in the late afternoon and darkened the valley.

On Mount Purgatory (*Purg.*, v), Dante is accosted by the spirit of Buonconte, the Aretine chieftain, who tells him how he was wounded and crept away to hide; but he was engulfed by the storm that swept his body into the valley stream, the Archiano, whence it was carried along and dumped into the Arno.

> The saturated air was turned to water,
> the rain fell . . .
> and as it changed into great torrents,
>> it rushed so swiftly towards the royal
>> stream
>> that nothing held it back.
> My frozen body at its mouth the raging
> Archiano found,

and swept it into the Arno, and
loosed the cross
upon my breast.

Dante in exile wrote a letter to the Florentine authorities (now lost but quoted from
by Leonardo Bruni, the fifteenth-century
biographer of Dante), in which he cited his
participation in the battle of Campaldino
"in which the Ghibelline side was almost
completely destroyed and dispersed, in
which I showed myself no child in armed
warfare, in which I felt much fear and at the
end great happiness over the outcome of the
battle."

The Florentines were back in their city by
July 24; but scarcely three weeks later the
priors dispatched another force, this time
about fifty miles westward to the neighborhood of Pisa. It was a smaller army, com-
prising perhaps four hundred horsemen,
including Dante, with a few thousand men
on foot. The aim was to besiege the castle
fortress at Caprona, a dozen miles inland
from Pisa, and restore it to its previous
Guelph resident Nino Visconti.

The Pisan story had undergone various
twists and turns in the 1280s. Long a
Ghibelline stronghold, the maritime republic had been subdued in 1284 by the

combined efforts of Florence, Genoa, and Lucca — a league organized by Brunetto Latini. Count Ugolino della Gherardesca was installed as ruler; but he soon conspired with the Ghibelline archbishop of Pisa, Ruggieri degli Ubaldini, to consolidate his power by ousting his own nephew Nino Visconti, who had resided in the tower at Caprona. The canny and ruthless archbishop then betrayed Ugolino, getting him thrown into prison with two sons and two grandsons.

There all five of them died, in a slow and horrifying process described to Dante by Ugolino in one of the chilliest sequences in the *Inferno*. In the lowest circle of Hell, Ugolino is seen gnawing endlessly on the head of Archbishop Ruggieri. He tells Dante how the children died of starvation, one by one, and how at last "Hunger was stronger than grief," and Ugolino fell to eating the young bodies.

Nino Visconti fled to Florence, where he became friendly with Dante, and at Nino's urging the small Florentine battalion undertook to recapture the fortress at Caprona. It loomed above a massive rock formation, about ten miles east of Pisa, in a country area filled with quarries (many of them active today). Adjacent is the village of

Caprona, small and attractive, if (today) a trifle dilapidated. Below, the Arno swirls and curves, and it was the ancient charge of the fortress to guard the river crossing at that point. A contingent came down from Lucca, twenty-five miles to the north. The siege lasted ten days, during which all supplies to the castle were cut off. Finally, the troops inside made signs of surrender, and they were allowed to come out unharmed. It was that tense and dangerous moment which Dante remembered in narrating a fearful personal moment, infested with demons, in the *Inferno*:

> Thus once I saw the footmen, who marched
> out under treaty at Caprona, frightened
> at seeing themselves among so many
> enemies.

four

The Death of Beatrice and a New Life: 1288–1295

We may go back a year or two, to the moment when the screen-lady departed for a distant city. Dante, riding away one afternoon on a short journey, was visited by another vision of Love: of that being whom he regarded, or pretended to regard, as a separate entity, but which he gradually acknowledged to be a fantasizing part of himself. Love, this time, was dressed as a poor pilgrim, and he had new counsel to give. What Dante needed, he said, was a follow-up screen-lady, "who will be your defense as was the first one." Love named his candidate for the role, and Dante recognized her at once. He then set about courting her so openly and insistently that people began to talk reprovingly about him. Hearing such talk, Beatrice, passing Dante in the street one day, withheld her greeting. Dante was stricken to the core.

One senses in Beatrice's behavior a certain maturity of mind, even a slight hardening of character. It was probably due to her new state, the married state. At some time in late 1287, so it seems, Beatrice Portinari was married to Simone de' Bardi and went to live with him in his family home in the Oltrarno.

The Bardis were a highly successful merchant clan, experts in banking and woolmaking. Their houses and towers stretched along a street — it is now called Via de' Bardi — that curved upward from the Ponte Vecchio area, running parallel to the river and then descending to a point near the Ponte Rubiconte. The Bardis would experience grave trouble forty-odd years later, when a pointless entanglement with young Edward III of England led to bankruptcy. Half a century after that, Cosimo de' Medici, principal founder of the Medici dynasty, was happy to take as his wife Contessina de' Bardi.

Beatrice at twenty-one was the second wife of Simone de' Bardi. She brought with her as dowry six hundred lire in gold florins, four times the amount Gemma Donati contributed for marrying into the Alighieri family. Beatrice now lived, not virtually next door, but on the far side of the Arno, and Dante had to walk through town and across the river to catch glimpses of her.

Meanwhile, wandering in a haze of self-reproach, Dante had still another vision of

Love, on this occasion as a young man dressed in white. Love tells him — or, as we may say, Dante now told himself — to stop playacting and instead write "certain words in rhyme" to Beatrice herself, words that would make clear "how you have been hers ever since childhood." Dante responded with *"Ballata, i' voi,"* which begins:

Ballad, I want you to seek out Love,
and go with him before my lady,
so that my excuse, which you must sing,
My Lord may then recount to her.

"She who must hear you," the ballad continues, "as I believe is angry with me." Love must tell his lady that Dante has been steadfast from the first in his love for her, and "never has he strayed."

To this, Dante added the sonnet "All my thoughts speak of love." Then, by chance, a friend came by to take Dante to a local gathering. A number of young ladies had come together in the house of a newly married woman: it being the custom in Florence, Dante explains, for ladies to keep a bride company "the first time she would sit at the dining-table in the house of her new bridegroom." As he stood there gazing at the group, Dante felt a tremor seize him, so strong that he had to lean back against a painting that covered the wall behind him. The seizure was caused by his suddenly recognizing Beatrice among the ladies. The others, observing Dante's condition, began to make fun of him among themselves, and evidently Beatrice joined in.

When he had recovered somewhat, Dante wrote a grieving sonnet about the experience, *"Con l'altre donne mia vista gabbate"*:

> With the other ladies you mock my aspect;
> and you do not think, lady, whence it comes
> that I resemble a figure so strange
> when I behold your beauty.
> If you knew it, Pity could
> no longer hold against me her wonted obstinancy . . .

In two further sonnets, Dante tried to explain his condition. "When I come to see you," he says in the first,

> My face shows the color of my heart;
> which, failing, leans wherever it can,
> and through the intoxication caused by great trembling,
> the stones seem to shout "Die, die."

The second one concludes:

> . . . I struggle, seeking to help myself;
> and all pale, of all valor empty,
> I come to see you, thinking to be healed;
> and if I raise my eyes to look,
> in my heart arises a tremor
> that from my pulses causes the soul to
>   part.

These lyrical excursions, be it remembered, were written at the times — 1287, 1288, 1289 — and under the circumstances described by Dante. It was only later, in the mid-1290s, that they were brought together in the work called the *Vita Nuova*, an extraordinary composite of poetry and narrative, and given their places in Dante's account of his love of Beatrice from her childhood to her death.

In the wake of these three confessional sonnets, and after considerable inner debate, Dante arrived at a major turning point in his life. It also comprised the first of two critical turning points in the *Vita Nuova*. The narrative is particularly rich in these portions (sections XVII–XIX) and may be quoted from at some length.

Because of the discouraging reception of the poems addressed to Beatrice, Dante says, he resolved to "keep silent." He would no longer speak directly to her. He would, instead, "take up new matter," something "more noble than the previous. And because the reason for taking up the new matter is delightful (*dilettevole*) to hear, I will recount it as briefly as I can."

He then tells of encountering a company of young ladies one day, Beatrice (he noticed carefully) not among them, and heard one of them call him by name, and ask why he continued to love Beatrice, since she made him so unhappy. Dante replied:

"Ladies, the end of my love was indeed the greeting of this lady, of whom you are perhaps thinking, and in that greeting lay my beatitude, for it was the end of all my desires. But because it pleased her to deny it to me, my Lord Love in his mercy has placed all my beatitude in that which cannot fail me."

The ladies murmur among themselves, amid many sighs, until his interlocutor asks Dante to explain where the new beatitude lies. And Dante answers, "In words that praise my lady."

He had said it: his happiness now lay in writing poetry in praise of his lady. But he held back for some time, fearful of making a poor beginning. Then one day, as he walked down a road with a stream running alongside, it occurred to him that he should speak of Beatrice only by speaking to other women — to gentle ladies and "not just women." There came into his head an opening phrase: *"Donne ch'avete intelletto d'amore."* Back home, he pondered this phrase for some time before beginning the canzone that, by any reckoning, was his first genuine poetic triumph.

The first words may be quoted in Dante's Tuscan Italian:

Donne, ch'avete intelletto d'amore,
i' vo' con voi de la mia donna dire,
non perch'io creda sua laude finire,
ma ragionar per isfogar la mente.
[Ladies who have an understanding of
    love,
I wish to speak to you of my lady,
not that I believe I may exhaust her
    praise,
but to converse to ease my mind.]

Dante sets the tone of his song of praise:

And I do not wish to speak so loftily
as to become through daring inept,

but will speak of her gentle estate
with respect for her discreetly.

In the second section of the seventy-line canzone, Dante, as he says in his gloss, tells
"what is understood of [Beatrice] in heaven"
— "The lady is desired in highest heaven" —
and "what is understood on earth":

when she goes along the way,
into villainous hearts Love casts a chill,
whereby all their thoughts freeze and
perish.

In the last section, Dante sends his poem on
its way:

Canzone, I know that you will go forth
speaking
to many ladies after I have released
you . . .
Strive, if you can, to open yourself
only to ladies and to men of courtly
ways.

There is a fluidity and grace in the poem
(as may well be detected in Dino Cervigni's
beautifully attuned translation) beyond
anything Dante had yet written, and a fresh
vitality of language. The canzone may be

said to have inaugurated a new mode of lyric poetry in Italy: the *dolce stil nuovo* as it came to be called. The phrase is that of Dante, who puts it into the mouth of the poet Bonagiunta da Lucca, with whom he converses on the next to last terrace of Purgatory. Bonagiunta asks him if he is the one who "invented the new rhyming, beginning with *'Donne ch'avete intelletto d'amore.'*" Dante in reply offers a classically high-toned expression of himself: "I am one who, when Love inspires me, takes note, and, in the manner in which he dictates within me, goes setting it out" (*vo significando*). Now, says Bonagiunta, he understands what it was that held him and others back from "the sweet new style (*dolce stil nuovo*) of which I have heard."

Dante himself named as his most honored predecessor in the new style Guido Guinizelli of Bologna, a poet who died in exile (he was a Ghibelline adherent) in 1276. Dante never knew him in real life, though during the short visit Dante paid to Bologna in the fall of 1287 (seemingly), he could talk with poetic affiliates and students of Guido, be directed to his poems, and absorb the atmosphere in which he had flourished. But Dante does meet him in Purgatory (xxvi), not long after the exchange with Bonagiunta. The figure comes forward with a singularly engaging self-identification: *"Son Guido Guinizelli e già mi purgo"* [I am Guido Guinizelli, and already I purge myself] (the English is less rhythmic). Dante addresses Guido as his father, *padre mio*, joining him with Virgil and Brunetto Latini in the visionary paternity. He adds that Guido was also the poetic father of others better than himself, no doubt thinking of Guido Cavalcanti and Lapo Gianni. Why, asks Guinizelli, does Dante hold him so highly? And Dante answers:

> your sweet songs
> which so long as modern use shall last
> will make their very ink precious.

"Modern use" (*uso moderno*) was none other than the sweet new style, which in Dante's lifetime succeeded the Provençal and Sicilian styles, along with that of the voluminous Guittone d'Arezzo — with their various characteristics of languidness, hardness, or obscurity — that had dominated lyric poetry in Italy for many decades. The leading voices in the *stil nuovo* were the Florentines Guido Cavalcanti, Lapo Gianni, and Dante, as Dante declared on many occasions, and never more sweetly than in the sonnet already quoted: *"Guido i' vorrei che tu e Lapo ed io. . . ."*

The new style practiced by these three, following Guido Guinizelli of Bologna, was poetry in praise of the loved one, without a trace of bravado, totally bereft of irony or double-edged wit, and emanating from "the gentle heart." Love and the gentle heart — this is the very theme of one of Guinizelli's best-known poems:

> *Al cor gentil rempaira sempre amore . . .*
> [The gentle heart betakes itself always to
>   love . . .]

Dante echoed the thought in a sonnet composed at the request of a friend (Forese Donati, perhaps), who had been much moved by Dante's canzone *"Donne, ch'avete intelletto d'amore"* and who wanted Dante to tell him more simply "what love is." The sonnet's opening lines:

> *Amore e 'l cor gentil sono una cosa,*
> *sì com il saggio in suo dittare pone,*
> [Love and the gentle heart are but one
>   thing,
> even as the sage pronounces in his
>   poem.]

Dante, speaking to the sage Guinizelli in Purgatory, refers to Guinizelli's "sweet songs" (he calls them *detti,* which might be translated "sayings"), and the musical charm of his new sonnet is further tribute to his forerunner.

We have arrived at mid-fall 1289. Dante had gone through an exceedingly active summer, on the battlefield at Campaldino and in the siege at Caprona, with the strenuous preparations and journeying for the two events. The military exploits, however, found no immediate outlet in his poetry, though war memories would recur in the *Comedy.* It is as though Dante's spirit now cherished something far removed from the derring-do of war. The sweetness and gentleness of the new poetry, that is, was an aesthetic reaction to the months preceding. But Dante in his young manhood — he was now twenty-four — was increasingly given to vibrantly shifting impulses, to major changes of attention. His emerging greatness as a personality lay partly in the coexistence of these large divergent impulses and in his capacity to move his whole being from one to another. The American reader may think perhaps of Walt Whitman, who could perform simultaneously or successively as a poet of cosmic range and unexcelled inventiveness, as an uncannily shrewd commentator on the drift of social and political democracy, as a lover, and as a recorder of war.

External events, of course, affected Dante's shifts of focus. He wrote a sonnet elaborating on the theme of the now famous canzone and with the same musical lilt:

Ne li occhi porta la mia donna Amore . . .
[In her eyes my lady brings Love,
whereby is ennobled everything she
looks upon.]

And then, not many months later, Dante learned of the death of Folco Portinari, Beatrice's father and a man, Dante said, who was "in the highest degree good." We know from existing records that Portinari died on December 31, 1289.

From this moment on, death is the countertheme with love in the *Vita Nuova*. Death had made an appearance earlier, in section VIII, when a young woman friend of Beatrice's had died and Dante duly wrote a commemorative sonnet, "Weep, lovers, since love weeps." But after Portinari's demise, death is a constantly lingering presence up through the actual death of Beatrice herself, only six months later.

Dante felt called upon to write some lines for the heartbroken daughter of Portinari, and he contrived two sonnets, the first and more compelling of which begins:

You who bear your aspect downcast,
with eyes lowered, showing sorrow,
whence do you come that your color
appears changed into pity's own?

"A few days after that," Dante related, "it happened that in a part of my body I was seized by a dolorous illness, from which continuously for nine days I suffered bitterest pain." We may question the "nine days" — every arithmetical calculation in Dante's writing is a multiple of three, by astrological necessity — but it was a drawn-out illness and may have been something like rheumatic fever. He falls prey to feverish fantasies of death — his own death, announced by a horde of disheveled women, then the death of Beatrice — "dead lies our lady" — followed by visions of darkening skies, earthquakes, birds falling to the ground — the end of the world.

But even as he wept fever-clouded tears, Dante had another vision, of Beatrice in heaven, with a look of such humility and peacefulness that Dante calls out, "Sweet

Death, come to me, and be not unkind, for you must be noble." He comes slowly back to reality, to find "a lady, young and gentle," standing at his bedside weeping with compassion. It is his sister (her name has vanished), one "joined to me by the closest blood relation" (rather than his half-sister Tana).

The other ladies ask his sister to leave, and in answer to their questioning, Dante gradually reveals the entire "false imagining," as he calls it, holding back only the name of Beatrice.

When he had fully recovered, Dante wrote a canzone about what had happened to him, alluding at the start to his grieving sister:

> *Donna pietosa e di novella etate,*
> *adorna assai di gentilezze umane . . .*
> [A lady compassionate and young,
> richly adorned with gentle qualities]
> who was there, where often I called on
>   Death,
> seeing my eyes filled with pain,
> and hearing my empty words,
> was moved by fear to bitter weeping.

The canzone chants its way through eighty-four lines, and before it is through

Dante has told again of his sickbed experience, his "false imagining" (he repeats the phrase) of his death and Beatrice's and the end of all things, and then the extraordinary transformation of vision and spirit when Beatrice appears to him sublimely at peace, with Death as something sweet and noble.

This is the second crucial turning point in the *Vita Nuova*, and, it is not too much to say, in Dante's understanding of the meaning of life and death. Francis Fergusson provides the compelling insight: that in a radical departure from the romantic medieval tradition of love and death identified together "with the mystic sweetness of night and the void," Dante now *welcomes* and praises death as the passage into immortality. "At the end the sweetness of death signifies his faith in Beatrice's immortality," Fergusson says, "thereby bringing about a reaffirmation of the human being, and restoring the poet to the waking world with a new sanity."

The new sanity expressed itself in a series of happy-hearted sonnets, and, following the first of them, in a discourse on the nature of poetic language. Dante had imagined Love as a human being, approaching him in the street, smiling and talking. He now knows perfectly well that Love is not a separate entity but something emanating from the soul, and that it is the privilege of poets writing in the vernacular to use such fanciful figures — so long as they can explain them. He and Guido Cavalcanti, Dante says, are familiar with some poets who fail to explain and "rhyme senselessly."

The third sonnet is particularly captivating.

> *Tanto gentile e tanto onesta pare*
> *la donna mia quand' ella altrui saluta*

The words delicately resonate:

> So gentle and so honest appears
> my lady when she greets others
> that every tongue, trembling, becomes
>   mute,
> and eyes dare not look at her.

The winter of 1290 passed, and the spring, and there arrived the day when Dante learned that Beatrice really had died. By one of his most complex calculations, invoking the Syrian calendar (which began in October) and "the perfect number nine" being completed "nine times," Dante tells us that Beatrice died in June 1290. He will not in this place dwell upon the event, because his language would be inadequate "to deal with it properly."

He did compose a tearstained poem, a "rueful canzone," as he called it, and bade it go from him, weeping, to find the ladies left disconsolate by the death of Beatrice. After this he was visited by one of Beatrice's brothers, who had apparently become one of the poet's best friends, for whom he wrote a sonnet purportedly about the departure of some other lady.

But after an interval, Dante did more than write an occasional poem of memorial grief; he put together the work to which he gave the title *La Vita Nuova di Dante Alighieri*. It was essentially an act of compilation, probably begun in 1293 and finished two years later. Dante drew up a narrative account of his relationship with Beatrice Portinari, from his first sight of her at the May Day party in 1274 to her death sixteen years later, sprinkling through it the poems — canzones, sonnets, a ballad — written to enshrine each successive moment. A few of these poems may have been written in the 1290s, in order to complete the presentation, but most of them were composed at the times described.

But "Dante the maker" (to borrow the title of William Anderson's very fine study) was wholly in command as the compilation took shape, and the result is a beautifully paced work, rhythmically rising and falling, with a prologue and three main acts. In the prologue, Dante recounts his first two meetings with Beatrice, through the epochal greeting in 1283. The first act comes to its climax in section XIX with the canzone *"Donne ch'avete intelletto d'amore"*; the second reaches its peak with the canzone *"Donna pietosa e di novella etate"* in section XXIII. The third portion, deliberately indecisive and perhaps a little overextended, passes through the death of Beatrice and its aftermath.

A little more than a year after Beatrice's death, while Dante was sitting in some public place, thinking painful thoughts, he happened to look up at the building opposite. "I then saw a gentle lady, young and very beautiful, who from a window watched me so compassionately, to judge by her look, that all pity seemed to be generated in her." Before long, Dante found himself addressing a sonnet to the window-lady:

My eyes saw how much pity

had appeared on your face . . .

In the days following, Dante sought out the unnamed young woman, until sorrowful appreciation turned to positive desire and delight. It is an unexpected but humanly understandable episode — Beatrice will scold him roundly for it when they meet in the Earthly Paradise (an important stage in the long process, acted out in the *Comedy*, of Dante's self-confrontation) — but aesthetically unclear. It lasts through sections XXXV–XXXVIII, until Dante argues himself out of the obsessions. He is now visited by a powerful new imagining: the vision of Beatrice as she was on that first May Day, "With the crimson vestments in which she first appeared before my eyes."

The poetic story is now complete; the Dante of 1274, entranced observer of Beatrice, is merged with the Dante of 1295, memoirist, poet, lover. He resolves "to write no more of this blessed one until I could more worthily treat of her." Should God permit him to live long enough, he will "say of her what was never said of any other woman." After this foreshadowing of some enormous poetic endeavor, the work ends with the inscription:

HERE ENDS
THE
NEW LIFE
OF
DANTE ALIGHIERI.

The new life is above all the life of Dante as a poet; one who has found in the writing of poetry the great purpose of his existence. In his new state of being, his understanding has been fortified as well by the vision of life eternal.

five

The Way of Politics:
1295–1302

Despite his disclaimer toward the end of the
Vita Nuova and despite a good deal of inner
torment, Dante continued to court the window-lady, with poetry and ardent glances
(and even, perhaps, a secret encounter or
two) for more than two years. The relationship reached a climax with a canzone — captivating but enigmatic — written late in the
year 1294. It began:

> *Voi che 'ntendendo il terzo ciel movete,*
> *udite il ragionar ch' è nel mio core,*
> *ch'io nol so dire altrui, sì mi par novo.*

It is addressed to the angels, or intelligences,
who through their act of understanding
(*intendendo*) move the third heaven, that of
Venus:

> [You who by understanding move the
> third heaven, listen to the argument that
> is in my heart, which I know not how to
> say to others, so strange it seems to me.]

The argument tells again of the conflict in Dante's soul between his grief over the departed Beatrice and his attraction to the "beautiful woman" (*bella donna*) who had so profoundly transformed his life. A new spirit of Love tells Dante to observe how full of pity and how humble the lady is and urges him to take her to his heart — "Resolve to call her your lady henceforth."

In the *Convivio*, the discourse on poetry and knowledge written during the early years of his exile (1306–1308), Dante tells of composing the canzone "*Voi che 'ntendendo.*" He says that it had indeed to do with the "gentle lady of whom I made mention at the end of the *Vita Nuova*" and recalls the long battle between the pull of the new love "and that which ran counter to it, and still held the fortress of my mind on behalf of that glorious Beatrice." But he now maintains that what he discovered during the period of suffering and searching was nothing else but philosophy; and that in the canzone he wrote about the experience, "I imagined her as made in the *likeness* of a gentle lady; and I could not think of her in an actual form as anything but compassionate."

There seems virtually no doubt that the window-lady was a very real person and that

Dante was strongly drawn to her, even while condemning himself for it. Through all the mists of a romantic literary tradition, real human beings, especially women, make their appearance in the *Vita Nuova*, as they did in Dante's young life. The fictionalizing of the window-lady in the *Convivio* was itself an act of fiction, one suited to Dante's self-characterizing purpose at the moment.

But it remains true that Dante came to the reading of philosophy in the time after Beatrice's death. Turning to philosophy for consolation, he inevitably found himself immersed in the *De Consolatione Philosophiae* by Anicius Manlius Severinus Boethius. Written in his last years, in prison at Pavia (he died there in 524), it is a work of prose, interspersed with poetry, describing how, through philosophy, the soul finds ultimate comfort in a vision of God. (Dante would find the treatise still more personally important when he reread it in exile, himself under sentence of death.) Dante, as he records, also found nourishment in Cicero, particularly his essay on friendship, *De Amicitia*, where there is wise counsel about the loss of a loved one.

Thus refreshed intellectually, Dante went on to study the theologians, beginning with a stay at Santa Maria Novella, the Dominican center whose church and cloisters lay just outside the western stretch of the old wall-circuit. Here he was instructed in the writings of Thomas Aquinas, the learned Dominican monk who had died in 1274 as he was finishing his masterwork, the *Summa theologica.* This prodigious text, which incorporated and in effect Christianized the recently rediscovered philosophy of Aristotle, supplied the basic doctrinal structure of the *Comedy.* Dante later spent time at the Franciscan center of Santa Croce, on the other side of town, and was guided through the mystical treatises of Bonaventura, among them his account of the "journey of the mind to God," in a phrase that became the title of his most influential work. From Bonaventura, who took to himself much of the visionary thought of St. Augustine, came the mystical strain in the *Comedy*, which everywhere pervades and gently modifies the toughly realistic philosophizing of Aquinas.

All these figures appear in the *Comedy* in person. Aristotle is seen early on, permanently settled in Limbo, where he is identified by the phrase "the master of them that know." Thomas Aquinas is met with in Paradise, in the heaven of the sun, where he names other kindred souls nearby, Boethius among them, who "from martyrdom and exile came to this place." Aquinas the Dominican then sings the praises of Saint Francis of Assisi and the Franciscan order, though ending with some harsh words for the contemporary representative of his own order. Bonaventura follows, prompted to speak "of the other leader," Dominic, because he had made "such fair utterance" about Saint Francis. He eulogizes Dominic, his learning and staunch fight against heresy, but he too regrets the current degeneracy of his fellow Franciscans. He ends by announcing himself: "I am the life of Bonaventura of Bagnoreggio."

Dante's readings in 1292–1294 bore fruit for the rest of his creative and intellectual life. If at the end of the *Vita Nuova* he had become a poet, one dedicated to the lyrical praise of love, he was now something richer — culturally speaking, something more substantial: a poet who commanded the language and ideas of the major classical schools of philosophy and the theological ranges of the thirteenth century.

Not long after the completion of the *Vita Nuova*, Dante's always pressuring and sometimes wayward imagination took a radical turn, one that testified to a certain inner turmoil but also carried implications about his future. As though in temporary repudiation of the sweet new style he had been practicing and praising, Dante suddenly engaged in an exchange of scurrilous sonnets, three on each side, with Forese Donati. If Guido Cavalcanti was Dante's "first friend," Forese Donati (probably a few years older than Dante) was the one whose company he most enjoyed, with whom (one fancies) he went carousing, and relayed gossip, and joked. One day, without any known provocation, Dante sent Forese a sonnet that spoke darkly of the incessant coughing "of the luckless wife of Bicci, known as Forese" (a slurring reversal of his friend's given name and nickname). "The coughing and other troubles," the sonnet goes on, were not due to bad "humors" but, rather, to Forese's failure to attend to her sexually — to "the gap she feels in the nest." Her mother is heard saying — here Dante puns on an enduring Tuscan vulgarity about the female sex organ — that the daughter should have married the aged but wealthy Count Guido of the Casentino.

In the *Purgatorio* (xxiii), as we will see, Dante did his best to make up for this slander. But here he is merciless; and in the two sonnets following he accuses Forese not

93

only of marital ineptness but also gluttony (for which in fact Forese is doing penance on Mount Purgatory), thievery ("people who carry purses keep clear of him"), probable illegitimacy, and servility before those who mistreat him.

Forese in turn denounces Dante as a sluggish (*ozioso*) layabout, living off the charity of others and from his father's usurious transactions. He cites an incident in which Dante should have leaped to the defense of his father, when somebody blackguarded the older man for usury, but Dante was an abject coward. Out of sheer terror, the sonnet announces, he defecated in his pants an amount such "that two packhorses could not carry it."

In the Dante annals, this episode is known as a *tenzone*, or dispute. It did not last very long, and Dante and Forese were warm friends again by the time of Forese's death in 1296. But the unsavory diction and scabrous allusions marked, in their way, Dante's reentry into the world of the mundane, after the heavenly visions of Beatrice. For Dante, poetically, it was an exercise in the "low style," a well-known literary mode of satiric and polemical nature. Socially, it heralded a return to the realities, often rough and grimy, of the here-and-now Florence — a new attention to what was happening around him, on the street corners of the *sestiere* of San Piero Maggiore and across the city at large.

It is less surprising that in the next phase of Dante's life, beginning around the middle of 1295, we see him stepping into the urban political scene. Here too his poetry played a role, as he lets us know in *Paradiso* viii. In Venus, the *terzo ciel*, a spirit approaches Dante, reciting the opening line of the canzone *"Voi che 'ntendendo il terzo ciel movete."* It is Charles Martel, of French royal descent, who had heard the poem sung at a happy gathering in Florence in March 1294, during a three-week visit Charles was making to meet up with his father, King Charles II of Naples. His quick understanding of the poem's obscure allusions and his full appreciation of its beauty endeared the visitor to Dante and, in doing so, gave impetus to Dante's entrance into public life. Charles Martel was the titular king of Hungary, "the land the Danube waters," as Dante has him say; and he had some claim to the throne of southern Italy. He arrived in Florence on March 5, riding up from Siena accompanied by two hundred knights in armor, clad in scarlet and green. This visit was a civic love feast, and as the historian Filippo Villani narrates, "the Florentines treated [the king] with great honor, and he showed great love for the Florentines." It was also a cultural festival. Charles listened responsively to performances of music and poetry and was escorted to the studio of the painter Cimabue, where he was allowed to see the artist's recently completed portrait of the Virgin Mary, a work that so enraptured the Florentines (legend has it) that they carried it around the city in a triumphal procession.

It seems likely that Charles and Dante talked seriously together about political matters. In Paradise, Charles, as though picking up a former topic of conversation, asks forthrightly:

> Now tell me,
> would it be worse for a man on earth
> were he not a citizen [*cive*]?

Dante answers at once:

> "Yes," I replied, "and here I ask no
> reason."

Their encounter led Dante to envisage Charles as the leader who would pacify and unite Italy and the Continent. But one year later Charles died in Naples, of the plague, at the age of twenty-three. "The world below held me but little time," Charles laments to Dante in Paradise. Even so, Dante, himself now age thirty, felt that the moment had arrived to take on civic responsibilities.

In 1295, perhaps around midyear, Dante inscribed himself in the apothecaries guild of Florence. He was, of course, neither a physician nor a pharmacist, though he had studied these subjects as portions of natural philosophy. But it was a guild hospitable to literary and intellectual folk; Dante was listed as a "Florentine poet."

It was another critical moment in the city's public life. In March of that year, Giano della Bella, author of the Ordinances of Justice (and a neighbor on Via del Corso), was driven into exile; he died two years later in France. The Ordinances, which came into effect in 1293, excluded members of the nobility and families of ancient wealth from having any part in the city government, and exacted severe penalties for harassment by a noble person or a "magnate" of a common citizen. In severe instances, a guilty magnate could have his hand cut off. Over two years, more than seventy members of noble families suffered the less painful punishment of exile. But in 1295, Giano became the victim of a skillful plot in which he was accused of treachery, and he fled the city.

Having had a hand in that plot, in alliance with the inevitable Corso Donati, was the recently elected Pope Boniface VIII. The former Cardinal Caetani had come into power in December of the previous year via a process that brought to an end one of the great sad dramas of medieval history — and that would have crucial consequences for Dante.

In the summer of 1294, the cardinals in Rome, wrangling hopelessly among themselves over the choice of a new pope, came to the unexpected decision to elect an Abruzzese monk named Pietro da Morrone, who spent much of his time in a cave in Mount Morrone. It was a lunatic idea, as has been said; the cardinals had to crawl up the mountainside in the Abruzzi to greet and prostrate themselves before the new pontiff. But the act was probably dictated as much by religious hope — Pietro was a saintly figure, wholly devoted to the poor and wretched in his reign — as it was by internal politics. But once in Rome, Pope Celestine V proved himself woefully incompetent. Within five months, he had abdicated, the only pope in history to do so, baited and maneuvered by the pope-in-waiting, Cardinal Caetani, who was soon invested as Boniface VIII.

Dante called Celestine a quitter, making out his shadowy figure early in the *Inferno*, just inside the gates of Hell, among the trimmers, those who never became fully alive, and labeling him the one "who from cowardice made the great refusal." For much later generations of Abruzzese mountain folk, among them the novelist Ignazio Silone, Celestine has been the greatest character in their history, and his canonization in 1354 has always seemed entirely fitting. But for Dante, Celestine's refusal (*rifiuto*) paved the way for the ascendancy of Boniface, a brilliant strategist possessed by a dream of absolute spiritual and secular power, who eventually connived to banish Dante from Florence forever.

There were almost literally countless civic opportunities for an energetic and ambitious young man in the Florence of 1295. Giano della Bella's Ordinances had been rapidly curtailed, but the government was still essentially middle-class republican. At the head were the three priors, drawn from the major guilds and housed across the way from the Alighieri house, in the Tower of the Castagna. Below them were a series of councils (*consigli*), varying in size from thirty-six to three hundred, and composed of citizens who discussed and debated (the Florentine love of argument was never more richly gratified), made proposals, and passed votes. Because of the peculiarities of scheduling and limitations of term, there were close to two thousand openings on the councils available every year.

Dante moved ahead at an impressive pace. Existing records show that Dante addressed the special council of the captains of the twelve major guilds as early as December 14, 1295; and in June 1296 he is found holding forth to "the council of the hundred." His topics of discourse are not mentioned, but one may well suppose that, even by Florentine standards, Dante was unusually eloquent. His reputation at a later date, as will be noted, was of one so persuasive in discourse as to be unnerving. There are no extant records for the following few years, but Dante must have gained in political strength and acumen, for in June 1300, he was elected a prior and moved into the Tower for two months of civic authority.

During these public years, Dante continued to lead a private and family life. His civic duties, after all, took him for the most part no farther than the fortresslike building, about a three-minute walk, called the Palazzo del Capitano del Popolo (the Bargello), the home of the captain, or elected representative, of the people. This building, according to an inscription on its wall, was to provide a setting for men capable of governing the city with a jocund heart (*governare la città con cuore giocondo* in the charming original phrase); and Dante for a time sought to do just that. Meanwhile, in the reasonably spacious home next to San Martino del Vescovo there resided Dante and his immediate family; the loving sister of unknown name, who came to his bedside during a grave illness in early 1290; his half brother Francesco, with whom Dante grew closer by the year; and a half sister Tana (Gaetana).

Of the four children of Dante Alighieri and Gemma Donati the oldest, Giovanni, appears to have been born in 1288; and so, when Dante talked to the council of one hundred, he was eight years old. The others were spaced about a year apart: Pietro, Iacopo, and Antonia. It was a harmonious family, by all evidence. Gemma was a patient and devoted wife, who cast a tolerant eye on Dante's imaginative erotic forays; and she supported their daughter when, in 1320, the young woman came to Ravenna, where her father was living, entered a convent, and took the name of Beatrice.

There were money problems, less than Forese Donati scornfully suggested in the *tenzone* but not unimportant ones in a Florentine world where the acquisition of money, moneylending, and banking were primary elements. The family income, under Dante's guidance, came entirely from property rentals, chiefly of the farmlands in Camerata, below Fiesole, and even more in Pagnolle (the farm here was called La Radere), which was rich in olive groves, vineyards, and fruit trees. There was also apparently a piece of city property in the parish of San Antonio, just outside the walls. Half brother Francesco was the one to handle these affairs, while Dante was writing his poetry or casting his vote in the councils. Francesco was diligent and scrupulous, handing over the proceeds periodically to the head of the family. But expenses outran these rentals, and in 1297 Dante had to float a substantial loan, for which his kindly father-in-law, Manetto Donati, and his mother's father, Durante degli Abati, stood as guarantors. A little later, Dante borrowed about 130 florins directly from Manetto, and in 1299 Francesco managed to scrape up a loan of 125 florins.

These transactions were not uncommon, and the ease with which they were carried through testifies both to Dante's good standing in the community and to his good relations with his in-laws. So much may be kept in mind when we come, as shortly, to the bitter conflict between Dante and his wife's cousin Corso Donati. They also help account for the near obsession with money — with greed and financial corruption — displayed in the *Comedy*.

The discord that gradually convulsed Florence, as the thirteenth century gave way to the fourteenth, originated in a neighborhood brawl. It began not in political disagreement but in simple family feuding. At one point in the mid-1290s, for example, the Donatis, a family of proud descent, observed the nearby palazzo of the Cerchis, a very wealthy but more recently arrived clan, being walled and heightened to overshadow their own. There were fisticuffs in the streets between youngsters from both families; and Corso Donati — who had once, typically, been married to a Cerchi — was heard to speak scathingly in public of the Cerchis (pigs and asses were his recurring references).

Guido Cavalcanti joined the fray. That elegant poet and cultivated nobleman was also hotheaded and prone to violence; he sided vigorously with the Cerchis and soon became the most visible member of that contingent. Seeing him as a threatening figure, the Donatis conspired to assassinate him. The attempt failed, but Guido, learning of it, organized a small cavalry band and rode down upon Corso Donati, coming along the street, and sought to stab him with an arrow. That effort failed too, but it was from events such as these that the area became known around town as "the *sestiere* of scandal."

Things grew more troubled. At a May Day dance in 1300, a brigade of young Donatis engaged in bloody combat with a cluster of Cerchis, and before it was over Ricoberino de' Cerchi, a lad of perhaps sixteen, had his nose cut off. "That blow," writes Dino Compagni in his chronicle of Florence, "was the destruction of our city." Six weeks later, on the 24th of June, the feast of San Giovanni, while the leaders of the guilds were marching through the streets, they were assailed verbally by a large group of magnates, Donatis and others, who shouted, "We won at Campaldino, but you keep us from the offices and honors we deserve!"

The time had come, the priors agreed, to take action. The two clans were now clearly divided into war-making parties, and they took or were given names borrowed from a similar period of strife in Pistoia: Whites and Blacks. The Cerchis and their allies were the Whites, the Donatis and their adherents were the Blacks.

Dante's personal affections lay with the members of the White faction (though he was also married to a Donati); but he was coming to believe that the welfare of Florence transcended these squabbles and even these private loyalties. Before the month was out a number of Whites were sent into exile, Guido Cavalcanti among them. A similar number of Blacks, most conspicuously Corso Donati, were banished. The minutes of the priors' discussions do not exist, but it appears that Dante made the key proposal and that he argued fluently in its favor.

Corso Donati was sent down to Castel della Pieve, on the southern edge of Tuscany; but he speedily disobeyed the injunction and fled south to Rome, where he began to consort with useful future comrades-in-arms. As to Guido Cavalcanti, he was assigned to Sarzana, in western Tuscany, about ten miles below the coastal town of La Spezia. His health declined; the distance from his native city seemed insuperable. From Sarzana, he wrote a hauntingly wistful poem to his loved one and sent it to her in Florence:

Perch'i' non spero di tornar giammai,
ballatetta, in Toscana . . .
[Because I do not hope to return
ever again into Tuscany, little ballad . . .]

The ballad must go in his place. In the twentieth century, T. S. Eliot, American-born, self-exiled to England, about to accept conversion to the Anglican faith, found poetic impetus in Guido's opening line and refurbished it with a mix of Shakespeare, for the opening of his own poem *Ash-Wednesday* in 1930:

Because I do not hope to turn again
Because I do not hope
Because I do not hope to turn
Desiring this man's gift and that man's
    scope . . .

As it happened, Guido Cavalcanti did return. He contracted malaria — a common disease in marshy coastal areas — and was permitted by some momentarily kind-spirited authority to come back to Florence, where he died before the year was out. Dante the pilgrim, talking with Guido's father in the *Inferno* in the spring of 1300, could not yet know of his friend's imminent death.

Following his two months in the Signoria, and largely because of his performance during it, Dante became a recognized leader in Florentine political life. According to Boccaccio, who may have been exaggerating in his well-intentioned way, no action was taken by the city council, no law was passed or abrogated, no issue of war or peace was decided unless Dante had his say. His position was steadfast: no yielding to pressure from the Donati Blacks or the Cerchi Whites, no involvement with external affairs. The welfare of the commune must come before everything.

The skimpy records show Dante addressing this council or that with impressive regularity and effectiveness; in the Brunetto Latini image, he had become the literary man *engagé*. Other important civic responsibility was put upon him. In late April 1301, he was appointed superintendent of roads and road repairs in Florence and was instructed to bring in supplies for such works from the country; the document hints at city-barricading, perhaps against an invasion by the displaced nobility. Earlier that month, Dante had spoken and voted in vain in favor of a proposal to have four priors in the Signoria for each *sestiere,* as against two. Then on June 19, he rose to discuss a request from Pope Boniface VIII.

The matter involved some extensive territories south of Siena that the pope wanted to get his hands on. The lands belonged to Margherita degli Aldobrandeschi, known as the Red Countess, whose marriage with the pope's nephew Goffredo Caetani had been arranged by Boniface himself. But Margherita was a wayward female; she had gone through two previous husbands and continued to consort with her lover Nello dei Pannocchieschi. Worse than that, Nello, in order to be free to cohabit with Margherita, had murdered his wife, Pia Tolomei, in their castle in the Sienese Maremma.

Ascending Mount Purgatory, Dante is approached by Pia, among the other late repentants (and after listening to Buonconte da Montefeltro's tale about his death at Campaldino; see Chapter Three). With disarming simplicity, her almost childlike spirit says:

> . . . *son la Pia;*
> *Siena mi fé, disfecimi Maremma:*
> [I am Pia;
> Siena made me, Maremma unmade
> me.]

Eliot borrowed and transformed these lines, too, in *The Waste Land*, a poem otherwise soaked in Dante. A voice at the end of "The Fire Sermon" declaims:

> Highbury bore me. Richmond and Kew
> Undid me.

Taking stock of all this, Boniface now arranged for a divorce between his nephew and Margherita. But he still lusted for the Aldobrandeschis' lands and had even ignited a local Tuscan war to achieve this goal. One more factor in the ongoing story was Cardinal Matthew of Acquasparta, whom Boniface had sent to Florence the year before, charged with bringing peace between the tumultuous Black and White parties. The cardinal was so obviously working to help the Blacks that an attempt was made to assassinate him (by a bolt from a crossbow), and the cardinal withdrew in haste. But it was he who, in June 1301, transmitted the papal request for armed support, two hundred horsemen, to help secure the southern Tuscan territories.

As of this moment, Boniface was not ill disposed toward the Florentines or toward Dante in particular. They were good Guelph citizens, in his view, resolutely opposed to the Ghibelline imperialists. During the jubilee year, a vast event that Boniface had launched with a papal pronouncement in February 1300, it seemed to him, as he said, that almost all the spokesmen for the myriad embassies to the Vatican were Florentines by birth. Florence, he was heard to say with an air of astonishment, was the fifth element in the cosmos. Dante was among his city's representatives in one of the two missions to Rome in 1300, either just before or just after his priory service; so, as of the following June, he was well in the pope's good graces.

At a first meeting on June 9, two members of the council spoke in favor of granting the cardinal's request. One moved that the question be postponed; Dante alone spoke up against it. "About the papal matter," reads the Latin report, "Dante Alighieri advised that nothing be done." *Nihil fiat:* that phrase, "that nothing be done," is attributed often enough to Dante in documents from 1300 to 1301 to give a clear sense of his staunch resistance to what seemed to him wrongheaded demands upon the city's resources. As it turned out, at a second sitting, on June 19, military support was offered to Boniface by a vote of forty-nine to thirty-two, an indication that the Cerchi-led White Party was anything but unified. But with his negative statement, Dante incurred the pope's severe displeasure.

In 1301, a new danger appeared on the Tuscan horizon: Charles of Valois, of the same house as Charles of Anjou, who had defeated Manfred and the Ghibellines at Benevento thirty-five years before and helped inaugurate the Guelph regime in Florence. The second Charles was a lackluster personality, constantly in need of money, always taking the easy way out. But Boniface believed that Charles could help establish French power in Sicily and also, perhaps, stimulate the Florentines into actively backing papal needs. He invited Charles into Italy. In May 1301, the French warrior with his troops stopped at Parma, where he borrowed a large sum from the Este family. Warily circling Florence, he continued on to Anagni, southeast of Rome, where in September he met the pope, worked him for two hundred thousand florins, and started back northward. At Siena, he kept an appointment with Corso Donati, and they began to plan their arrival in Florence.

The threat of Charles of Valois was debated before a full council meeting on September 13 and again two weeks later. Dante spoke out both times. On September 27, he was effective in gaining a vote to declare the complete innocence of one Neri Diodati, wrongfully accused of sanguinary violence; and then the council turned again to the French presence. Dante evidently voted his opposition to any compromise.

By October 4, Charles had reached Castel della Pieve, where the exiled Donatis were awaiting him — all except Corso, who was in Siena by this time. The priory hastily appointed a three-man embassy to go down to Rome, with the mission of persuading the pope of their complete Guelph loyalty and begging him to call off Charles of Valois. The three ambassadors were Maso Minerberti, Corazzo Ubaldini, and Dante Alighieri. The ambassadors met with the pope and made their pleas. Two of them were then released and sent back to Florence; Dante was detained.

He was not in the city to witness the fearful events of November 1301. On November 1, Charles of Valois entered Florence with a retinue of two thousand horsemen. He promised the White Priory to preserve the peace but instantly turned the town into an armed camp. Corso Donati was permitted to return. He stood near his home in San Piero Maggiore shouting curses and vengeful threats, then led a band through the *sestiere* looting and burning. The Alighieri house was vandalized, and the family fled to the home of a nearby relative. The sitting priors were deposed, and on November 8 a new set of priors, all Black, was elected, and a new *podestà,* Cante de' Gabrielli di Gubbio, always favorable to the Donatis, was called back from exile and placed in charge.

Cardinal Matthew of Acquasparta made a genuine effort to calm things down, but he was scorned and ridiculed and finally chased out of the city. New violence broke out, in the course of which Corso Donati's favorite son, Simone, attacked Niccolò dei Cerchi, his uncle (the brother of Corso's first wife); both were killed. The entire White contingent had left Florence by the start of April.

Florence was entirely in the grip of an all-Black priory, under the vindictive new *podestà.* The ever active Corso Donati roamed the streets, handing out punishments to lingering Whites, with the forces of Charles of Valois virtually occupying the city.

It was the new priory that on January 27, 1302, issued a detailed condemnation of Dante Alighieri and three others on charges of financial corruption. Dante was charged both in his capacity as head of the program of road repairs — pocketing funds and accepting bribes — and during his time as prior, with what we would now call campaign financing irregularities, and other crimes. For not answering these charges, Dante and others were subjected to enormous fines and two years' banishment from public office. On March 10, 1302, the priory, prodded by their superiors, issued the ultimate condemnation: Dante and now fourteen others were condemned to death by burning.

Dante had been held at Rome until these developments were well under way. He began the journey back to Florence and reached Siena when he was informed of the accusations in the decree of January 27th. He seems to have understood at once that it would be fatal for him to present himself in Florence to plead his case. He remained outside the city, to learn shortly of the final condemnation.

His ancestor Cacciaguida, talking to
Dante in the planet Mars in April 1300
(*Par.* xviii), two years before these calami-
ties, predicts them with sad accuracy:

. . . You will be severed from Florence.
So it is willed and already plotted,
and will be accomplished soon by him
who preaches there where Christ is put
   to sale every day.

Dante, writing fifteen years later, thus
puts the major blame for his grief and that of
Florence on Pope Boniface VIII. But he
knows that for a time he himself will be the
one accused of wrongdoing:

The blame will fall upon the injured side
As always.

Yet hope remains:

Vengeance shall bear witness
to the truth which dispenses it.

But Cacciaguida's 1300 vision of Dante's
future is a grim one:

You shall abandon everything you love
   most dearly.

That is the arrow which the bow of
    exile
shall shoot.

It was an arrow that reached its mark. Dante never again set foot inside the city of Florence.

six

The Poet in Exile, 1302–1310: The *Comedy* Is Begun

For a time following his banishment and the death sentence, Dante moved about restlessly, mostly within the confines of Tuscany, keeping a watchful eye on developments in Florence. It was a dismally disorienting period. Cacciaguida warns Dante about it in *Paradiso* xvii: "You shall abandon everything most beloved," and in addition, "You shall discover how another man's bread tastes of salt." For Dante, as for Florentines today, salted bread was a kind of punishment. But there were flickerings of hope.

In early June 1302, Dante joined with sixteen other White Guelph exiles in an alliance with the Ubaldini family to plan an invasion of Florence. The Ubaldinis — Ghibellines by tradition, and vigorously opposed to the Black Guelphs of the city — resided in the tiny hill village of San Godenzo in the Mugello, some thirty miles northeast of Florence. It was a picturesque region of farms, chestnut trees, and olive groves, and was already becoming a summer home for the wealthy, with the Sieve River running south through it. The Mugello had the added appeal for Dante of belonging to the same countryside as the Alighieri holdings of fond memory at Pagnolle, just over the hills to the west.

Two months after the alliance was formed, the Florentine Blacks, taking note of it, sent a somewhat disorganized force to attack the exile group. The latter repelled the onslaught easily, their only military achievement during this entire phase of things. Early in 1303, Dante gave up on the Mugello coalition and continued on his northeastern course, ending up at Forlì, a flourishing town of Roman origins (the name derives in part from the forum that once stood there), now ruled by Scarpetta Ordelaffi, another Ghibelline adherent. His family would command Forlì for two hundred years. Scarpetta quickly enlisted Dante as an advisor on political and military matters; but after six months Dante took off again, making his way up to Verona, as emissary of the local White Guelphs to the Veronese leader Bartolomeo della Scala.

It was the beginning of a long relationship, perhaps the most valued of any in Dante's exile years. Cacciaguida reports in advance on it:

> Your first refuge and your first place of
>   rest
>   Shall be the courtesy of the great
>   Lombard, who
>   On the ladder bears the sacred bird.

The della Scala family arms showed an eagle on a ladder, a *scala*, hence the name (the older German name, often invoked in Italy, was Scaliger). Alberto della Scala had died in 1301; he was succeeded by the oldest of his three sons, Bartolomeo. Between the new ruler and Dante, as Cacciaguida perceives it, there grew an ideal friendship: each, Cacciaguida says, gave first, gave freely, and only then made any request.

On this first visit, Dante remained in Verona about nine months. Bartolomeo honored and protected him; and the exile seems gradually to have felt almost at home in the city. It was a compact town of artful design, like Florence, with a river, the Adige, curving gracefully through the heart of it, even as the Arno flowed through Florence. Rolling green hills surrounded Verona, as they did Florence; and within the walls were reminders that Verona, like Florence, was a "daughter of Rome" — most visibly the vast Roman amphitheater, the Arena, rivaling in bulk the Roman Colosseum and dominating the urban center and the river view.

Dante's mission in Verona was to gain the support of Bartolomeo della Scala for another White Guelph effort to force their way into Florence. In late 1303, the moment seemed propitious. The French monarch, Philip IV, "the Fair," had quarreled with Boniface over the matter of taxation and had been summarily excommunicated. In furious revenge, Philip sent two henchmen to the papal palace at Anagni, thirty-five miles southeast of Rome. They seized and manhandled Boniface and plundered his palace — the moment became known as "the terrible day at Anagni." Boniface died in Rome a month later, in October. For all his hostility to Boniface, Dante denounced the attack as mortally sinful, an attack against Christ Himself. In the *Purgatorio* (xx), Dante speaks of seeing "the fleur-de-lis enter Anagni, and in the person of His Vicar, Christ being made captive." But he was understandably relieved to see Boniface depart, and he rejoiced at the election of the mild-mannered Benedict XI.

Hope arose when Benedict sent an able diplomat, the cardinal of Prato, to Florence, with the aim of effecting a truce between the

Blacks and the Whites. Dante addressed an open letter to the cardinal — it is his first surviving letter — on behalf of the "Council of the White Party," declaring their belief in the papal emissary and their high expectations.

But the endeavor came to nothing: the Blacks were intractable, and the cardinal left Florence in June 1304, having placed the city under a papal interdict. Benedict himself died in July 1304; the complex politicking within the college of cardinals led to a hiatus in the papacy for eleven months, after which time Clement V was elected. The papacy was controlled by the French during the rest of Dante's lifetime.

Dante had left Verona by the early spring of 1304. The cardinal's mission was evidently doomed to failure, and Bartolomeo della Scala had died that winter. He was succeeded by his brother Alboino, with whom Dante was unable to get along. In the *Convivio* (IV, xvi), the work he would soon set about writing, Dante would refer scornfully to Alboino as one whom some people thought of as noble simply because he was well known. Eventually, of course, Dante would come within the orbit of Alberto's youngest son, Can Grande, but that future ruler was no more than a stripling of thirteen when Dante quit Verona.

The departure from Verona symbolized an act by Dante that was the product of extreme frustration and impatience: a sharp and final break with the White Guelph exile group. In retrospect, and once more via Cacciaguida, Dante labels them "wicked and stupid" (*malvagia e scempia*), "completely ungrateful, mad and impious." They were leaderless and inept, a motley unorganized crew, who on their side appear to have accused Dante of slack performances as an emissary. Dante now struck off entirely on his own — in Cacciaguida's phrase, he made "a party for yourself" (*parte per te stesso*).

It was as a party of one that Dante went on to Padua briefly, and then to Bologna for a longer stay. Among the poets and scholars of Bologna, Dante to his joy met up with his friend Cino da Pistoia, a poet and jurist about five years younger than Dante and (what did not trouble Dante in the slightest) a member of the Black Guelph party in his native city. He had been an exile from the time of the White party takeover of Pistoia.

Dante and Cino had exchanged sonnets, often with accompanying letters, for a good many years, talking mainly about poetry and the poetic idiom and about the vicissitudes of love. Typically, in one of the earlier verses, Cino had asked Dante's advice about how he should respond to a new and lovely lady he had come to know, the "green lady" as he called her. "Dante, what shall I do [*Che farò, Dante*]?" Dante's sonnet, in reply, observed somewhat enigmatically that "there is great danger in a woman so clothed" — in green — "so in my opinion you should call off the hunt."

In Bologna and immediately afterward, Dante and Cino each passed at least three sonnets back and forth until sometime in 1306, when Cino was able to return to Pistoia. The poems are personal, affectionate, and literary. Dante grows reminiscent: "I have been together with Love since my ninth year," he tells Cino, who had asked about how Love and desire might be controlled, "and I know how he curbs and spurts, and how, under his sway, one laughs and groans." And, in a flash of self-exposure, "He who urges reason and virtue against him acts like one who raises his voice in a storm."

One of Cino's sonnets followed Dante across Italy to the region of Lunigiana, in the northwest tip of Tuscany. To this ancient and still thriving Roman settlement Dante came in 1305, at the request of the

Marchese Malaspina, who had heard of his diplomatic skills and besought him to intercede in a harsh dispute with the local power figure, the bishop of Luni. Dante settled the affair quite satisfactorily, and it was then that there arrived the communication from Cino, punning on the name Malaspina by lamenting that an evil thorn (*mala spina*) had pierced his heart. Could help be sent him before he died? To this, Dante responded in a fondly chiding tone:

> Your sweet and clear voice makes you worthy
> to find any treasure, but your fickle heart
> where the bard of love never made a wound
> leads you away from it.

Cino's last surviving sonnet to Dante speaks mordantly about his condition of exile, but then brightens at the prospect of a new beauty available for love. Dante again scolds him amiably:

> One who falls in love as you, now here, now there . . .
> shows that love wounds him but lightly.

Before offering that nugget of wisdom,

however, Dante struck a surprising new note:

> I thought, Master Cino, that I had quite abandoned
> this poetry of ours, for now my ship
> must hold a different course, being further from the shore.

He will comment briefly on Cino's philandering, Dante says, but after that he will be otherwise occupied.

This sonnet was probably written in Lucca, the old walled city thirty-five miles due west of Florence. In his new commitment to the party of the self, Dante had come to realize that though he was still a Florentine — "native and citizen" of the city, as he continued to say emphatically — he was above all a Florentine poet, or better, a man of letters. He was ready to embark, to borrow his own metaphor, upon new poetic ventures: and first a prose study of poetry, especially Italian and Tuscan and Florentine poetry; more largely, of the language of poetry and of language in general and historically. Such was the large aim of *De Vulgari Eloquentia*, the treatise on vernacular poetry that he began in Lucca — a singularly fitting place, it might be added, since the Lucchese have often been said to speak the purest Tuscan of all.

The work emerges directly from the Bologna days with Cino da Pistoia. Dante's sonnet from the Lunigiana spoke of Cino's "sweet and clear voice"; there is a similar allusion to Cino's "sweet words" (*dolci detti*) in the sonnet following; and, conspicuously, in *De Vulgari Eloquentia*, Dante points more than once to him as a rare example of what Tuscan poetry can hope to achieve at its finest.

Before arriving at those accolades, Dante offers a survey of human language — something only human beings are capable of and that is the basis of common human life — from the single language of Adam through the infamous Tower of Babel, which brought a chaos of languages into the world, down to the (then) present time. Three major groups of language can be observed (the number three, as always, frames the analysis): northern, eastern, and southern. Of the latter, there are three main groups: French, or the language of *oui;* Provençal, or the language of *oc;* and Italian, or the language of *si*. But Italian speech — very much like the ill-fated country of Italy, so Dante implies — divided rapidly into rival idioms. Not only do Pisans and Paduans speak differently, but so do people in neighboring cities and even people in different parts of the same city. All in all, Dante identifies fourteen separate Italian dialects. He has said at the outset that no one before him had ever attempted a study of this sort; and indeed, in its conceptual reach and empirical detail — Dante's remarkable ear had listened to and recorded differing accents in almost every corner of the land, apparently — nothing remotely like it had ever previously been undertaken.

Italian, even so, is the best of the existing languages, Dante contends, because the best poetry has been written in it. Here Dante pauses to denounce Tuscan modes of expression as in effect idiotic blather. But a few writers, he says, have reached excellence in the vernacular: and he cites "Guido [Cavalcanti], Lapo [Gianni], and one other [himself], all from Florence, and Cino da Pistoia."

The treatise moves on to a celebration of the lyric mode known as the canzone: the highest form of poetry, so Dante claims at this moment (c. 1305) in his career, the one that combines the best features of the ballad and sonnet. Most of Book II of *De Vulgari Eloquentia* is devoted to the canzone, the only poetic form capable of handling the lofty themes of poetry: heroism, love, virtue — these latter being further defined as boldness in arms, true passion, the righteous will. Among the few truly expert practitioners, Dante cites the Provençal poet Bertrand de Born (c. 1140–1215), who sang of war as the finest human pleasure:

> I tell you that I find less pleasure
> in eating, drinking and sleeping,
> than in hearing the cry of "Charge!" . . .
> and seeing the dead with bits of lances
> and banners protruding from their sides.

The warrior in Dante had admired this sentiment; nonetheless, in the *Inferno*, Bertrand is located far down in the eighth circle, swinging his severed head by its hair and confessing to having given evil counsel to young Prince Henry of England (pushing him to rebel against his father, King Henry II).

Dante also mentions Arnaut Daniel, who sighed in Provençal about the great love that had entered his heart, and for whom Dante had a high regard. Closer to home, he lists Cino as the Tuscan poet of love and as "the poet of righteousness." From his own work, Dante quoted *"Doglia mi reca ne lo core ardire"* [Grief brings boldness to my heart],

128

the opening line of a lengthy canzone that Dante had only recently completed and the next-to-last canzone he would ever write. It was intended as a poem in praise of liberality, but it consists mainly of a multipronged attack on the sin that most aroused Dante's fury: that of avarice.

For the rest, Dante identifies the *canzone* as tragic in nature, suited to "the superior style of poetry," whereas comedy was fit for "the inferior style" and elegy for "the style of the unhappy." A canzone should consist of stanzas of equal length. There are references to Guido Cavalcanti and Guido Guinizelli ("the great Guido"), and further presentations from his own writing, including several entries in the *Vita Nuova*, among them *"Donne ch'avete intelletto d'amore"* and *"Donna pietosa e di novella etate."*

Though its aim is to establish the validity of vernacular literature, the *De Vulgari Eloquentia* was written in Latin, as befitted an essay directed toward the learned. It ran to two books and about fifty pages (in a modern edition). The work was intended to run a great deal longer, but it breaks off at the end of chapter xiv of Book II; probably because Dante wanted to hurry on to a companion piece, the essay composed in the vernacular and called the *Convivio*.

By way of illustrating his claims for the canzone, Dante in the *Convivio* proposes to ex-
amine a number of canzoni he had written
over the years, though not without meditating
at some length on the propriety of an author's
talking so much about himself. The *Convivio*,
as its title indicates, is a banquet, a feast of
knowledge in which all men of goodwill are
invited to participate — on the assumption
that Aristotle was right when he said at the
start of the *Metaphysics* that all men by nature
desire to know. The food at this banquet will
be served in fourteen courses, as fourteen
canzoni, submitted for inspection and understanding. In fact, Dante analyzed only three,
and the treatise breaks off after four books
and about 250 pages.

The *Convivio* was written between 1306
and 1308. The first part may have been
written in Lucca, soon after breaking off *De
Vulgari Eloquentia*. The remainder may have
been put together "on the road." That itin-
erant condition is palpable in the text,
which is at once the most demandingly ab-
stract and the most openly personal of anything Dante had yet written. The personal
posture is exactly that of the forlorn wanderer, praying to be allowed back into his

proper home. This note is struck in the third chapter of Book I, where he speaks of having

> unjustly suffered punishment, the punishment, I mean, of exile and of poverty. After it was the pleasure of the citizens of that fairest and most famous daughter of Rome, Florence, to cast me out of her dearest bosom — wherein I was born and brought up to the summit of my life, and wherein with their good leave, I desire with all my heart to rest my weary mind and to end my allotted span — I have wandered through almost every region to which the tongue of ours extends, a stranger, almost a beggar . . .

To make matters worse, Dante writes, "Not only was my person held cheap, but every work of mine became of less esteem."

The *Convivio*, among its other intentions, is an elaborate effort to reestablish that lost esteem by demonstrating the high merit of the poems Dante had written and circulated over the years. But there is another note audible in the lament just quoted, the hint of an apology, or at least of a readiness to make an apology. The same note was sounded in *"Tre donne intorno al cor mi son venute"* [Three women have come round my heart], a canzone written during the Bologna days and introducing three women who identify themselves as Justice, Generosity, and Temperance. They are sorrowful and disheveled; Justice's dress is so torn that there is visible "that part of her which it is decent not to name." Like Dante, they are in exile, they have been driven from their home (Florence, presumably); they are "weary and abandoned by all." If these great qualities have been banished from Florence, Dante reflects musically, then he counts it as an honor to be exiled along with them. But he begins to wonder if he may not have been in small part to blame for what happened, and asks if he has not by now repented enough. So he sends the canzone back to Florence, with a plea to the Whites and the Blacks alike to forgive him:

> Song, go hawking with the white wings;
>   song, go hunting with
> the black hounds — which I have had to
>   flee, though they
> could still make me the gift of peace . . .
>   A wise man will not lock
> the chamber of forgiveness; to forgive is
>   a fine victory in war.

Whether the canzone, or "song," ever

reached Florence or was even glanced at there is not known, but no offer of peace resulted. At the same moment, Dante addressed an open letter to the Florentine people; the letter has been lost, but Lionardo Bruni quotes the opening sentence, the Gospel phrase, in Latin: *"Popule mee, quid feci tibi?"* [Oh, my people, what have I done to you?].

As the *Convivio* goes ahead, Dante measures his present poetic self against the self represented in the *Vita Nuova*. That work, he says, was written when he was entering his youth, and its manner was properly passionate and fervid (there is a trifle of self-fabricating here: Dante was close to thirty when he finished the *Vita Nuova*). The *Convivio* is composed by the mature man (entirely accurate), and so its style will be manly and temperate. It is in this spirit that Dante, in Book II, discussed *"Voi che 'ntendendo il terzo ciel movete,"* maintaining, as we recall, that the figure envisaged is not a flesh-and-blood woman but an allegorical image of philosophy.

Book III takes as its central text the canzone *"Amor che ne la mente mi ragiona"* [Love, speaking in my mind of my lady so reverently]. It is the poetry of praise, deliberately echoing the *dolce stil* of the *Vita*

Nuova; but now the lady is unequivocally philosophy or what philosophy leads to: Divine Wisdom, with which the human soul longs to be united. In the *Comedy*, Divine Wisdom takes the form of Beatrice.

Finally, in Book IV, Dante examines a canzone that announces at the start that it will not consist of love poetry but, rather, will employ "harsh and subtle rhymes" to study a practical question: what is the source of true nobility, of *gentilezza?* Dante calls this his "against-the-erring" poem (*contra-li-erranti*). Among the false notions it confronts is that nobility has anything to do with wealth; riches, the poem proposes, are themselves "base by nature . . . base and defective." Nor is nobility a matter of birth, as some mistakenly believe. True nobility arises from virtue; "nobility is wherever virtue is."

We recognize another large swing of Dante's mental and imaginative energy, from love and philosophy to the world of human affairs. In his commentary on the canzone, and in view of the enormous changes and challenges on the international scene at the time of writing, in 1307, Dante argues forcefully for the desperate need for a supernational state presided over by a single secular authority. Dante, in his political thinking, had moved beyond the city-state as the happiest context for human life; but he was still enough of an Italian to assume that the international ruler would be an emperor crowned in Rome. The discourse shows that Dante would be ready for the appearance in 1309 and 1310 of the human being who might fulfill this supreme role, Henry VII, the young king of Luxembourg.

Dante wrote one more canzone before he gave up the lyric mode altogether and moved to the vast epic enterprise of the *Comedy*. It is a fascinating, spirited, and tormentingly uncertain poem, known by its initial phrases: *"Amor, da che convien pur ch'io mi doglia"* [Love, since after all I am forced to grieve for others]. It was evidently written in the Casentino Valley; Dante addressed it as his "mountain song" (*montanina canzon*) and speaks in it of some extraordinary experience of love "among the mountains," along the banks of a river. Dante made the case clearer in a Latin epistle he sent to his former patron Malaspina of the Lunigiana, accompanying the poem. Here Dante apologizes for not having been of further service to his lordship (on some mission or other) and explains that he had

scarcely set foot along the fluid streams
  of the Arno,
when suddenly, alas, descending like a
  flash
of lightning from on high, there appeared a woman,
I know not how, delighting me with her
  appearance.

In the poem itself, Dante complains that he cannot get her out of his mind, or out of his poetry, so obsessed is he by "her beauty and malice" — malice, because of her disastrous effect upon him.

Dante instructs his mountain song, should it go back to Florence — "my city, that shuts me out from her" — to say that Dante is no longer belligerent: "My maker can make war on you no longer, he's bound by such a chain in the place I come from."

The lady who so convulsed Dante has been thought by some to be a real woman of the Casentino, toward whom he felt an overpowering carnal desire. Others have taken her to be Beatrice, appearing suddenly from on high in a vision that paralyzes Dante's whole being. But Dante was by now a writer who took joy in doing and saying two or more things at once. We may suppose that the Casentino lady was real enough — beautiful and tempting enough — to begin with; but that in Dante's imagination, as he was writing the poem, she began to change magically into Beatrice. It is a first glimpse, so to speak, of the Beatrice he will meet up with at the summit of Mount Purgatory, in the Earthly Paradise, heart-stirringly lovely and morally stern at the same time.

In this view, the mountain song marks the transition from impassioned lyric to visionary epic. The letter to Malaspina, narrating the origins of the canzone, was written in 1308 or 1309. The writing of the *Inferno*, by this reckoning, began in that period, somewhere in the Casentino.

"The author of the *Commedia*," says Francis Fergusson in his superior study of Dante (1966), "with its sustained movement, its freedom of style, its unparalleled wealth of concrete perceptions, is a new Dante." At some time between writing the *Convivio* and beginning the *Commedia*, Fergusson suggests, Dante underwent "a change of heart . . . a turn to a religious view of man and his fate." But Dante's religious view being what it was, essentially a mode of Christian humanism, Fergusson continues, "this meant freeing him as poet to represent the human with a subtle, many-sided realism that had no parallel in his time, and has not been surpassed since. . . . He can, for the first time, fill his poem with many spirits and many voices besides his own, and with all the sights and sounds and smells of 'God's world.' "

So he embarked on his otherworldly journey: down through the circling of the Inferno, where souls like Paolo and Francesca, and others much wickeder than they are doomed to eternal punishment; up the slopes of Mount Purgatory, where souls like Pia Tolomei are being purged of their sins and prepared for ultimate salvation; and into Paradise, where souls like Piccarda Donati live in eternal blessedness. We have no record of the successive phases of writing. But Dante's fabulous mind evidently carried the whole of the *Commedia* within itself from the instant of its inception.

"Nel mezzo del cammin di nostra vita" — in the middle of the journey of our life — such is the ever-echoing opening of the *Inferno*. It tells us that the adventure occurred when Dante was thirty-five years old; the span of human life was then reckoned to be seventy years. This means in turn that we are in the year 1300, eight or nine years before Dante wrote the line. We will learn that it is April

7, Thursday evening in Holy Week. The pilgrimage continues through Good Friday, the day of Christ's crucifixion, through Easter Sunday and the first few days of the week following.

Dante remembers finding himself "in a dark wood, where the straight way was lost." (Nothing in Dante's conduct in the early months of 1300 suggests a loss of moral direction; if any literal reference is intended, it is more likely to be the mid-1290s, when he flirted with the window-lady and wrote scabrous verses to Forese Donati.) As he now moves warily toward the foot of the hill — a means of escape, he hopes — he is confronted by three beasts who block his way: a leopard, a lion, and a she-wolf.

The animals, we gather retrospectively, are allegorical representations of the qualities and forces that have wrought destruction upon Florence and Italy and would lead to Dante's exile: lust, a special Florentine sin; ambition, the fatal flaw of the papacy; and avarice, for Dante the most unattractive and most common human failing. Fifty lines later, the poet alludes to another allegorical beast, a greyhound, who seems in some way to be the future redeemer of Italy, possibly the then nine-year-old Can

Grande della Scala.

An apparently human figure appears. He declares himself to be "not man, but a man I once was." It is Virgil, the Mantuan poet who sang of Aeneas. Dante greets him as "my master and my author," the one from whom he learned the style of writing poetry that has brought him honor. Virgil explains that a hard journey lies ahead of them. The threatening beasts prevent their ascending the mountain; they must take another way. Virgil will serve as guide through "an eternal place where you shall hear the hopeless shrieks" — the Inferno; then through the place assigned to "those who are contented in the fire, for they hope to come . . . among the blessed" — Purgatory. And last, if Dante wishes to ascend, "there shall be a spirit worthier than I to guide you" — Beatrice, who has sent Virgil to rescue Dante from the depths and who will escort him up into the heavens.

In the Dantean scheme, Virgil represents human wisdom, the quality that can guide the individual in the good life and make him worthy of redemption; and Beatrice is Divine Wisdom, which alone can disclose the truths of salvation and the life eternal. But here we must pause to consider the whole matter of interpretation.

The *Divine Comedy*, as it came to be called in English, has properly been subjected to endlessly varied modes and levels of analysis and commentary. Dante himself began the process in a letter to Can Grande, written in 1319, in which he declared his intention to dedicate the *Paradiso*, on which he was then working, to his former host and patron, in return for his kindness. The letter, so to speak, raises didacticism to high poetry. In lecturing fashion, Dante lays it down that the work in progress is twofold in nature, the treatise and the treatment; that the treatise is threefold (canticles, cantos, and verses); that the treatment is multifold (poetic, fictive, descriptive, and so on) — and more of the same. Here we may rehearse Dante's lucid insistence that the work is not a tragedy, a mode that begins in tranquillity and ends in horror, but rather a comedy, a mode that may begin with adversity but ends in happiness. The present poem takes its start in Hell but finishes in Paradise.

The *Comedy*, he says, is not limited to a single meaning but "might rather be called polysemous, that is, having several meanings." These latter divide first into two main kinds, the literal and the allegorical: the actual account of what happens to human souls after death, and what that account can mean in moral and theological terms. American literary criticism half a century ago, often citing the letter to Can Grande, was much given to discourse about the "four levels of meaning": literal, moral, allegorical, anagogical. It tended to interpret "allegorical" as indicating the general drift of human history, as Faulkner's novels might reflect the history of the South, and "anagogical," the fourth of Dante's categories, as the imagery of some ultimate metaphysical fact.

No literary work ever written yields more to this manner of analysis than does the *Divine Comedy*, with its hypnotic episodes and encounters and characters; its elaborate and always coherent moral scheme; its expansive views of what was happening to Florence, Italy, and Europe; and its Thomistically derived portrait of divinity. At the same time, Dante is the supreme example in literary history of the writer who, at every important turn, is seeking himself (humanly, morally, psychologically, imaginatively), finding himself, defining himself — in effect, telling his life story. In the present biographical context, these are the aspects of the *Comedy* that I will be emphasizing: most simply, the poetry of Dante's autobiography. We should keep in mind that the poem resonates on broadening levels of significance, and that the colossal achievement is composed of those resonances.

Although the drama of self-discovery is more evident and continuous in the *Purgatorio*, it is at work urgently enough in the *Inferno*. We may begin with the story of Paolo and Francesca in Canto v. Dante, led by Virgil, has by this time passed through the Gate of Hell, with its inscription:

> "*Per me si va nella città dolente . . .*
>   *Lasciate ogni speranza, voi ch'*
>   *entrate.*"
> [Through me is the way into the doleful city . . .
>   abandon all hope, you that enter.]

He has observed the trimmers, those who never came to real life, for good or evil, Pope Celestine V among them. They are a huge throng, and Dante is astonished: "I never believed that death had undone so many" (a line that comes into modern poetry via T. S. Eliot to Hart Crane). He has come into the first circle of Hell — Limbo is its other name, an antechamber of Hell — and seen there the good pagans, those who were never baptized (he will ask about them, and the justice of their placement, in Paradise). He has noticed especially the great ancient poets, "the lords of highest song": Homer, Horace, Ovid, Lucan. Virgil makes the fifth of these lords, and Dante is happy to record that they greeted him and made much of him, designating him as the sixth among them. The poet has seen heroes and heroines of antiquity — Electra, Aeneas, Caesar, Camilla; and the great philosophers — Socrates and Plato, and "the master of them that know," Aristotle.

With Virgil, Dante has passed into the second circle, where the infernal torment begins, and where carnal sinners are blown about by an unresting wind. Before it sits Minos, the horrific judge, who decides where each sinner, after confessing, shall be sent for eternal punishment. In a dark, storm-swept place within the circle, two spirits approach, and Dante hears their story. The one who speaks is Francesca da Polenta, of Ravenna. She was married to the lord of Rimini but fell in love with his younger brother, Paolo; the husband caught them in the act of lovemaking, and stabbed them both to death.

Telling of this, Francesca, as it were, rehearses the *Vita Nuova*, with its climactic poetry of love and death. She sings of love (*amor*), which is so swiftly caught in the *cor gentil* (gentle heart) and which needs no excuse. Love, she says, led the two of them to one death: *"Amor condusse noi ad una morte."* In Dante's Tuscan, the tonal repetition of *amor* in the phrase *una morte* is itself a version of the love-death theme and of the fateful human conjunction.

Dante is passionate to know how it all happened. And Francesca:

> *Nessun maggior dolore*
> *che ricordarsi del tempo felice*
> *nella miseria;* . . .
>
> [There is no greater pain
> than to recall a happy time
> in misery.]

(Dante, somewhere in Tuscany, is talking to himself here.) One day, Francesca relates, they read about Lancelot and his love for Guinivere.

> When we read how the fond smile was
>   kissed
>   by such a lover, he who shall never
>   be parted from me, kissed my mouth
> all trembling.

145

The book acted upon them like a Pandar — in the Italian word, a Galeotto:

Galeotto fu 'l libro e chi lo scrisse:
   quel giorno più non vi leggemmo
   avante.
[A Galeotto was that book, and he who
   wrote it.
      That day we read no further.]

Overcome by compassion for the two sinners, and by the warm remembrances of his own experience of love and death, Dante falls into a dead faint; and the gleamingly lovely sequence comes to an end.

Paolo and Francesca are in Hell forever; but theirs is the least venal of all the sins that bring departed souls into the Inferno — Dante stresses this more than once. Further down, in the sixth circle, for example, where the heretics are entombed (Canto xi), Virgil lectures Dante on the comparative gravity of human sinfulness. He cites a passage in the *Ethics* where Aristotle, in a discussion of incontinence, malice, and bestiality, argues (in Virgil's paraphrase) that "incontinence less offends God and receives less blame." Virgil advises Dante to think back to those in the second circle, above, who are being punished for carnality; and Dante will see how they are clearly separated from the wicked spirits far below them and "why, with less anger, divine justice strikes them." It is sound classico-Christian doctrine, in the ongoing humanistic vein, Dante's way of rendering a relatively mild judgment on his own behavior.

While still unconscious, Dante is carried down into the third circle, where he awakes to discover the souls of the gluttonous, lying prostrate in the mud, buffeted by foul water and snow. One of them sits up and calls to Dante; he is a Florentine citizen known only by his nickname, Ciacco (hog). Dante takes the occasion to ask for news of their city, whereupon Ciacco predicts the coming strife and the brutal victory of the Black Guelphs. Their 1300 colloquy in Hell is darkly stained by the poet's perspective of a decade later.

Descending into the fourth circle, Dante is confronted by the avaricious, countless numbers of them, all rolling dead weights and hitting each other. The time, apparently, is past midnight.

In the sixth circle, where the heretics are stretched out in fiery tombs, Dante hears a voice saying "O Tuscan . . . Your speech clearly shows you a native of that noble country" (Canto x). It is the Ghibelline leader Farinata degli Uberti, who raises himself until part of his body is visible. He and Dante hold the exchange quoted earlier, with Farinata recounting how he alone had saved Florence from total destruction. Another spirit cries out from the fires: Cavalcante de' Cavalcanti, who asks piteously about his son Guido.

From this scene, Dante is led down a precipitous path through loose-lying stones to a river of blood that flows about the entire seventh circle. Here the violent are severely punished, beginning with the violent against their neighbors such as tyrants and murderers. Next, the violent against themselves, the suicides, with that self-negating act adroitly introduced by three tercets beginning with the word *Non:* "Not green was the foliage," and so on. The most memorable of these sinners is Pier della Vigna, once the honored chancellor to Frederick II, as well as a competent writer of Latin prose and Italian poetry. He fell into disgrace, was blinded and imprisoned, and killed himself in 1249. The spirit ends his sad tale with a plea and a flash of poetry:

"E se di voi alcun nel mondo riede,
  conforti la memoria mia, che giace

148

ancor del colpo che 'nvidia le diede. "
[And if any of you return to the world,
　　give comfort to my memory,
　　　which still lies prostrate from the
　　　blow of envy.]

Deeper into the seventh circle, on its third level, Dante finds those guilty of "violence against nature." They are running across burning sand, and one of them, coming close, seizes Dante by the hem of his shirt and exclaims *"Qual maraviglia!"* It is Brunetto Latini, with whom Dante partakes of the dialogue previously explored, which continues until Brunetto takes his leave, running hard, and seeming to Dante like one in the annual race for the green cloth at Verona "who wins rather than one who loses."

In the same corner of the seventh circle, Dante has pointed out to him the grandson of "the good Guadralda," his remote kin Guido Guerra, who "in his lifetime did much with counsel and sword." In particular, this Guido counseled against the Florentine attack upon the Sienese that led to the Guelph disaster at Montaperti in 1260. There seems no explanation for why Dante has Guido Guerra being hurried along among the sodomites. But all thoughts of him are driven from Dante's head when he sees swimming upward through the air toward them "a figure marvelous to every steadfast heart." This is Geryon (the name is pronounced with a soft *g*), "the savage beast with the pointed tail," so Virgil tells Dante, "who passes through mountains and breaks through walls."

He is the very incarnation, "the uncleanly image," of Fraud (the sin next to be envisaged), with "the face of a just man" but a reptile's body, bearing two hairy paws. He is to be the travelers' transport down to the eighth circle. Before mounting him, Dante is urged by Virgil to look at the last batch of sinners in the present circle: they are the usurers, and Dante is careful to say, after looking into their faces, that he does not recognize any one of them.

The two climb onto the beast's back, Dante in front, Virgil behind him, clasping Dante in his arms; and the descent begins. Virgil gives strict military orders: "Now, Geryon, move yourself. Make your circles large and your descent gradual." Geryon swims downward slowly, circling and dropping, with Dante holding on tightly, too stricken with terror to be more than dimly aware of the dark evils flying about them.

> At the bottom, Geryon set us; close to
> the foot
>> of the ragged rock; relieved of our
>> weight,
>> he bounded off like an arrow from a
>> string.

That long spiraling journey downward through the fetid air, amid hovering unseen terrors, perfectly dramatizes a decisive turning point in the *Inferno*: from the serious but lighter sins of incontinence and violence all the fearful distance downward to fraud and deceitfulness — seducers, simonists, evil counselors, forgers — with the traitors to friends and country within the ninth, and lowest, circle. Dante's hierarchy of human misbehavior is altogether firm and coherent; to the modern mind, it is for the most part sane and sensible. What startles the imagination, moment after moment, is Dante's twisty inventiveness in the dramatic imagery invoked for the successive circles and settings, characters and misdeeds, particularities of torment. The author of the *Vita Nuova* and the *Convivio* had, through a miracle of self-development and through constant immersion in Virgil's *Aeneid*, become the grand master of dramatic narrative.

The eighth circle is named *Malebolge:* Evil

Chasms or, perhaps, Pouches. It is a circle of dark-colored stone divided into ten individual pockets of punishment, and occupying Cantos xviii through xxx, more than a third of the entire *Inferno*. Here Dante sees "new miseries" and "new tormentors," beginning with the souls of seducers and panders who are being scourged without letup by horned demons. One of them declares himself to be a Bolognese, and Dante's disaffection with that city's recent political history is conveyed in the observation that the whole place is packed with Bolognese. Dante's opinion of fawning courtiers, for him an especially distasteful form of fraud, is shown in the figure of Alessio Interminei da Lucca, whose head is smeared with excrement.

In another chasm, Dante notes with distinct approval those guilty of purchasing spiritual office, the simonists, implanted upside down in narrow round holes, while the soles of their feet are roasted. Here, Dante fancies, Boniface VIII will soon be placed, although the pope would not die until 1303.

The two poets pause at the edge of the fifth chasm and stare down into the darkness to make out souls covered with filthy pitch and being torn at by demons each time they show any part of themselves. These are the barrators, to use the old term, those who have misused public funds for private gain, an unhappily familiar sin in our day. It was the crime for which Dante was falsely accused and condemned by the Black Guelph leaders, and he regards the scene of retribution with so much fascination that he almost falls into the pitch. "Take care!" cries Virgil, as he pulls Dante back.

Virgil, as the adventure moves ahead, becomes a more recognizably human character at each stage. Dante salutes him as "my lord" and addresses Virgil as his good master and his guide. Virgil is all these things, even as, on a higher level, he is the embodiment of human sagacity and the voice of Aristotle. But he is also kindly and wise, with something of the good schoolteacher's attentiveness as well as his disciplinary rigor. No character in the *Comedy* is allowed to be purely allegorical.

When Dante inveighs against the simoniac popes (xix) — "your avarice grieves the world . . . you have made yourselves a god of gold and silver" — Virgil listens with a markedly satisfied look, then takes Dante in his arms and carries him up to the surface of the chasm. Not long after, Dante sees a cluster of demons coming toward them. His hair rises in fear, and he cries out to Virgil that he should hide them both. Virgil speaks soothingly to him, then takes Dante "as a mother . . . takes her child," sliding down the chasm wall with Dante sheltered in his arms. Dante is sufficiently restored by the Roman poet's parental care that he can respond at once when a group of spirits in slow procession, wearing heavy cloaks of gilded lead — they are the hypocrites — approach, hearing his Tuscan speech, to ask who he is.

> And I to them: "On Arno's beautiful river
>> In that great city I was born and grew."

Dante's dramatic power reaches a peak in the episode centering on Ulysses (xxvi). The old Greek warrior and strategist is the most handsomely endowed character in the *Inferno*, and the one whose story is as riveting as his ultimate fate is puzzling. This encounter begins with a deceptively pleasing image drawn from the poet's memory of his family's country home at Pagnolle:

> As many fireflies as the peasant, resting
>> upon the hill . . . sees down in the valley,

> where perhaps he gathers grapes and
> he tills . . .

The analogy is to the horrid spectacle of countless flames seen down below; they are wrapped around the bodies of sinners guilty of evil counseling, as they run along the rim of the chasm. Here as elsewhere Dante underscores the horrors of Hell by borrowing a charming image of the earthly world above.

Among these damned souls is Ulysses, condemned, as Virgil says, for his part in getting the Trojan Horse inside the walls of Troy. Since Ulysses is Greek, he cannot understand Dante's Tuscan vernacular, and Virgil addresses him in properly lofty tones. The enveloping flame shakes from side to side, and a voice from within then launches into a speech unmatched in the *Comedy* for its shapeliness of form and its dramatic idiom.

> "When I departed from Circe, who
> beyond a year
> detained me there near Gaeta . . .
> neither fondness for my son, nor rever-
> ence
> for my aged father, nor the love
> that could have cheered Penelope

could conquer in me the ardor I felt
> to gain experience of the world, and
> > of human
vice and worth."

So he put forth once again, on a single ship with a small company of men. They saw Spain and Morocco and the Pillars of Hercules. That would seem the utmost limit of human voyaging; but Ulysses exhorts his men to yet greater effort:

" 'Oh brothers,' I said, 'who through a
> hundred
> > thousand dangers have reached the
> > western rim,
> deny not to your brief life
experience of the unpeopled world
> beyond the sun.
> > Consider your origins: you were not
> > formed
> to live like brutes, but to follow
virtue and knowledge.' "

The crew is aroused to the point of exultation. They "turn the poop towards morning," and voyage on until they see, dim in the distance, the Mount of Purgatory. But here a terrible tempest arises. The winds seize the forepart of the ship:

"Three times it made her whirl round,
  with all the waters.
      At the fourth, it made the poop rise
      and the prow go down, as it pleased
      Another,
till the sea closed over us."

"Com' altrui piacque" — as it pleased Another. It is a classically stirring drama, with a classical culminating phrase. It is also a large moment in Dante's assessment of himself. He too had left behind wife and children and home to seek experience of the world; he too had gone in search of "virtue and knowledge." True, he had been ejected forcibly from his native city. But in a part of him he knew that ways, however humiliating, could be found to allow him to return to his family; and in another part, he felt that the endless pursuit of new experience was heroic to an extreme. (Tennyson's Ulysses, it can be noted, while deriving audibly from Dante's, is even more clearly cast in the heroic vein, as the well-known closing lines reveal:

      . . . that which we are, we are;
One equal temper of heroic hearts,
Made weak by time and fate, but strong
  in will

To strive, to seek, to find, and not to
  yield.)

The flame that was Ulysses falls silent and
goes away. Another being, wrapped in fire,
comes toward the travelers, making bel-
lowing sounds, like a bull. Virgil remarks
that this one is obviously an Italian, so
Dante can speak to him. Dante asks the
sinner who he is; the voice roars a little
longer, then quiets down and replies. His
first utterance, with its recurring "s"
sounds, catches the hissing noise of the
flames:

> *"S'i' credesse che mia risposta fosse*
>   *a persona che mai tornasse al mondo,*
>   *questa fiamma staria sanza più scosse. "*
> [If I thought my answer were made to
>   one
>   who could ever return to the world,
>   this flame
>   would shake no more.]

T. S. Eliot deploys the passage as the
epigraph for his poem "The Love Song of
J. Alfred Prufrock" (1917), giving the next
tercet as well to convey the sense of
Prufrock, the Boston wanderer, speaking
from a metaphorical world after death:

"Ma per ció che gia mai di questo fondo
non tornò vivo alcun, s'i' odo il vero,
senza tema d'infamia ti rispondo."
[But since no one has ever returned alive
from this depth, if what I hear is true,
without fear of infamy I answer you.]

The sinner is Guido da Montefeltro, a Ghibelline leader who had connived with Boniface against his own party, then was typically deceived by the pope. He had died in 1298.

In the ninth chasm of the eighth circle there are the sowers of discord, a horde of them, sources of bitter uprisings in their cities and communities. Dante despised them in life, but their punishment in Hell is almost beyond his ability to describe. One of them has his body ripped down to "where one farts"; his entrails hang between his legs. Another has his throat pierced and his nose cut off. Still another has both hands sliced away. He lifts his stumps and identifies himself: he is Mosca, who galvanized his family and their Amadei relatives into murdering Buondelmonte on Easter morning in 1216, barking *"Capo ha cosa fatta"* [Let's get it over with]. This, Mosca says mournfully, "was the seed of evil to the Tuscan people."

In the tenth chasm are counterfeiters and forgers, among them Adam of Brescia, who forged Florentine gold coins and was burned at the stake for it in 1281. He is miserably parched, and Dante the poet provides him with a tantalizing image of the fresh Casentino waters in the world above:

"The rivulets that from the verdant hills
    of the Casentino descend into the
    Arno,
    making their channels cool and
    moist
stand constantly before me."

Adam points to another falsifier nearby, Simon the Greek, who cunningly persuaded his Trojan captors to admit the wooden horse. He engages in a noisy dispute with Simon, in language so colorful that Dante is transfixed until Virgil reprimands him severely, saying that to want to hear such things "is a vulgar wish."

A horn sounds. In the mist, Dante thinks to see a number of high towers. They are giants sunk to their navels in a huge well and reminding Dante of the walled Tuscan town of Monteriggioni, with its circuit of fourteen towers. One of them, Dante discovers, is Nimrod, ruler of Babylon who, in the poet's mythology, built the Tower of Babel, splintering the one human language into many. Another is the giant Antaeus; it is he, Virgil informs Dante, who will carry the two of them down "to the bottom of all guilt," to the very base of Hell.

Virgil makes a bundle of Dante and himself; Antaeus takes hold of them. Looking up at him, Dante thinks of the leaning tower in Bologna:

> Such as the Carisenda seems to one's view,
>> beneath the leaning side, when a cloud
> is going over it . . .

(The words are inscribed at the foot of the Torre della Carisenda, as it leans against its twin, the Torre degli Asinelli, in Piazza di Porta Ravegnana in Bologna.) Dante rather wishes they could descend by some other means, but Antaeus carries them gently and sets them down on what Dante calls "the bottom of the universe." To describe the scene, Dante remarks, is anything but a sport.

He espies a frozen lake; encased in it, with only their heads and necks showing, are those who betrayed their kinfolk or their country. Walking past, Dante kicks one of them savagely in the face. This is Bocca degli Abati, an ex-Ghibelline who had seemingly joined the Guelphs at Montaperti but who, at a crucial moment, had cut off the hand of the Florentine standard-bearer. The Guelph disaster followed.

They had barely left Bocca, Dante narrates,

> when I saw two frozen
> in one hole so closely that the one head
> was a cap to the other.

They are Count Ugolino of Pisa and Archbishop Ruggieri of the same city, whose treacherous story has already been told. They are now packed close in the ice, with Ugolino gnawing at Ruggieri's head.

Silence surrounds Ugolino's long slow narrative (xxxiii, 4–75), an absence of sound the more chilling after the noisy cursing in the previous circle. So we hear of the children in the dungeon, of little Anselm pleading desperately, of little Guido crying out, "My father! Why don't you help me?"

> There he died; and even as you see me,
> so I saw three fall dead, one by one,
> between the fifth day and the sixth . . .

then hunger had more power than
    grief.

Along with the Paolo and Francesca sequence, and those of Brunetto Latini and
Ulysses, Ugolino's story is the greatest
poetic and dramatic moment in the *Inferno*.
Coming near the end, it counterpoints the
Paolo and Francesca story near the beginning. There two lovers are bound forever by
love; here two enemies are bound forever by
hatred. Dante is so moved by the tale told
by Francesca that he faints away. His reaction to Ugolino's narrative is cold silence,
except for a burst of anger against the city of
Pisa and the expressed wish that the Arno
would flood it. The hideous fate of the little
children may have grieved him; but
Ugolino, like Ruggieri, is an unredeemable
traitor.

The travelers move along to the final
spectacle. Dante sees many other traitors
buried in the ice:

Some are lying; some stand upright,
    this on his head, that on his soles,
    another like a bow bends his face to
        his feet.

So they come to Satan, the Emperor of the

Dolorous Realm. "Once as beautiful as he is now ugly," Lucifer, the light-bearer, is up to his waist in ice and so enormous as to make the giants seem small.

Satan has three faces; tears gush steadily from all six eyes. From one frozen mouth in front hangs Judas Iscariot, the archtraitor of mankind; from the two behind hang Brutus and Cassius, the betrayers of Julius Caesar and the city of Rome.

"Night is reascending," Virgil observes — it is the evening of Holy Saturday. "And now we must depart, for we have seen the whole." Dante holds his master from behind, by the neck, and they make their way down the final slope. They then "entered the hidden road, to return to the bright world." Their position is reversed as they leave the Inferno. Now they are climbing.

> We mounted up, he first and I
>   second . . .
>   And thence we issued forth again to
>   see the stars.
>   [*E quindi uscimmo a riveder le stelle*].

seven

The Middle of the Journey:
1310–1319

From the late summer of 1310 to the mid-summer of 1313, even as he was bringing the *Inferno* toward its conclusion, Dante's mind was again aroused by grand possibilities in the world of war and politics. He had made one of his recurring visits to the Casentino, this time as the guest of Count Guido da Batifolle in his castle at Poppi, the fortified hill town that dominated the enclosed valley (as it does today) from the southern slope. Directly below, as Dante could see by gazing down over the shoulder-high wall-circuit, was the plain of Campaldino, where he had ridden to victory with the Florentine cavalry two decades before. Now, perhaps, history was preparing a larger victory, via the figure of young Henry VII of Luxembourg.

The emperor's seat had been empty since the spring of 1308, when Albert I of Austria, who had some claim to it, was murdered by his nephew John of Swabia. Clement V, the French pope who, in 1305, had settled the papacy at Avignon, seemed to favor Henry for the imperial crown. Henry was in his mid-thirties, of modest estate (as the chroniclers would say of him), courageous, free of cupidity (in Dante's phrase), and magnanimous in spirit. As Henry, encouraged by the pope, prepared to enter Italy in September 1310, Clement issued a letter to the leaders of Italy and all its citizens, requesting them to welcome the new ruler and to obey him, proclaiming that Henry would come as a peacemaker.

This was likewise the theme of the rapturous letter that Dante composed in the Casentino in September 1310, dispatching it as from "the Italian Dante Alighieri, the Florentine, exiled counter to his deserts" and addressing it to all the princes and lords and people of Italy, foreseeing for them all the end of "our long calamity" and the looked-for joy when "peace-loving Titan shall arise, and justice . . . will revive again." In ever swelling rhetoric, Dante intoned, "O Italy, henceforth rejoice . . . Your bridegroom, the solace of the world and the glory of your people, the most clement Henry, Divus and Augustus and Caesar, is hastening to the bridal."

A month after that letter, in October, Henry entered Italy from the north. In January 1311, in Milan, he was crowned king of

Lombardy, in a ceremony Dante was able to attend. But Henry then made the tactical error of appointing a Ghibelline as his viceroy (imperial representative); and this at once enraged the Black Guelphs in Florence. They refused to acknowledge Henry or even to see him; Henry in turn showed himself reluctant to make any move against the city. Dante, tingling with impatience, now wrote two open letters to both parties: to the Florentines on March 31, 1311, and to Henry on April 16.

Both letters were composed in the Casentino, to which Dante had retreated after Henry's inauguration in Milan. He was now the honored guest of Count Bandino, in his ancient high-turreted castle, far up on the northern slope of the valley, "under the source of the Arno," as Dante put it in his letter to Henry. The river, as Dante would soon be describing in *Purgatorio*, has its origin a little farther up on Monte Falterona.

With his fellow citizens, Dante did not strive for a conciliatory tone. "Iniquitous Florentines," was his phrase for them; and he accused them of transgressing both human and divine law. He condemned them for their stupidity in refusing to open their gates to Henry VII as the true Holy

Roman emperor of Italy and Europe. The Florentine rulers seemed blindly unaware that "the triumphant Henry" pursued not his own good but the general good. If the Florentines persisted in their stance, Henry would invade and ravage the city; even the new circuit of walls would be brought down — "You shall gaze mournfully upon them as they fall."

For "the sacred and triumphant Henry," Dante has a no less urgent message: invade Florence at once. Florence was the true impediment to gaining control of Italy; the emperor's real enemy "does not drink of the headlong Po, nor of the Tiber, but his jaws pollute the streams of the torrent of Arno." He concluded, "Come then, banish delay"; and, in a customary biblical idiom, "slay this Goliath . . . and Israel shall be delivered."

It was probably sage advice, though we do not know if Henry VII ever saw the eloquent appeal. In any event, he held back from attacking Florence. He spent most of the summer and the early fall of 1311 in a lackluster siege of Brescia, fifty-odd miles east of Milan, in the Lombard war zone. At the start of 1312, Henry formally declared the Florentines to be rebels against the empire. In late June, Henry was belatedly crowned

Holy Roman emperor in Rome, in a ceremony of questionable validity: not in St. Peter's, the proper place, and not by the pope (who was huddled away in Avignon), but in the church of St. John Lateran, and by a cardinal from Prato.

In the spring of 1313, Henry moved into Tuscany and appeared to be preparing for an assault upon Florence. But he had lost something of his old determination, especially since the death of his wife, Margherita of Brabant (Dante had been in correspondence with this intelligent and forceful woman), the preceding fall. He pulled his army back to the Pisan area and went down to Siena. Here he contracted malaria and died of it on August 24, 1313.

About the time when, to Dante's perception, the imperial conquest of Tuscany seemed imminent, he issued a treatise on political philosophy called *De Monarchia*. He had begun it in the year 1308, when Henry of Luxembourg was just emerging as the likely and enormously desirable new emperor. Dante's political passions were rekindled. But the Latin prose essay, on true rulership, was in no way a diversion from the poetic work-in-progress. On an immediate and personal level, the essay had to do with the political conditions under which the epic might most effectively be carried forward.

At the heart of the first of the three books are several linked statements. It is laid down, first, that only in the "tranquility of peace" is "the human race," and every individual in it, "most freely and favorably disposed toward the work proper to it." Universal peace being thus the supreme goal of mankind, it can, second, be ensured only by a single and universal empire ruled over, third, by a single monarch or emperor. The "work proper" to Dante Alighieri was the writing of the *Comedy*; ideally speaking, only a universal empire and emperor could create the proper conditions for it.

Dante, as we have been seeing, wrote much of the *Inferno* on the move — even on the run — sometimes hungry and threadbare. But in his intellectual vision there loomed an epoch of universal tranquility, with everyone, himself included, getting ahead with the work ordained.

De Monarchia sprang as well from a corollary conviction that it was the duty of highly educated persons to speak out concerning urgent political challenges. This too is set forth early on in Book I, when Dante argues that anyone who has been imbued with "public teachings" — for Dante, primarily the *Politics* of Aristotle — but who does not seek to "contribute to the public good" has fallen far short of his duty. Dante was here discussing what in our time is called the public responsibility of the intellectual; he felt strongly about the matter, and no one has written more cogently about it. Deploring the idea of the "buried talent," he expressed his own deep desire to speak out "for the public advantage" and in the present treatise "to set forth truths unattempted by others." It was all very well, he remarked, for intellectuals to brood about questions they can do nothing about, questions in mathematics and theology, for example; "but there are some that are subject to our power, and that we can not only think about but do." The question at hand related to the best form of human society and hence was concerned "not with thinking but with doing."

In this spirit, Dante, in his characteristically encyclopedic manner (recall the history of human language in the *De Vulgari Eloquentia*), offers a survey of Roman history, drawing upon the *Aeneid*, and following that history to the age of Augustus and the incarnation of Christ. The great image and need of a universal empire are contained within that mythic pattern, as

Dante unfolds it. In Book III, he turns to the authority of the papacy in the universal scheme, and maintains that it extends only to spiritual matters and cannot impinge upon secular affairs. The declaration of Christ before Pilate is invoked: "My kingdom is not of this world."

Less than a year before the death of Henry VII, Dante had returned to Verona, where he settled more or less continuously from late 1312 to mid-1318, the longest stay in his exile years. It is from this period that we have our first verbal portrait of him, put together by Boccaccio from interviews with Dante's former associates. The poet, now about fifty, was of middle height and given to stooping a little. He had a long face, an aquiline nose, large eyes, a heavy jaw, and a prominent underlip. His complexion was dark. His hair and beard were thick, black, and crisp. Dante had grown a beard a good many years earlier. He walked in a grave and sedate manner, his countenance almost always sad and thoughtful. He was on all occasions and with all whom he encountered courteous to a degree.

Dante had become a not unfamiliar figure in Verona. Boccaccio tells of several Veronese ladies who saw him walking by one day. They were struck and a little frightened by his appearance, his face fixed in gloom and smudged as though by soot, his beard bristling as though tinged with fire. He seemed, they thought, a character emerging from his own Inferno.

That impressionistic reaction suggests, what we know from other sources, that Dante's *Inferno* had gained recognition by, say, 1315. The first known reference to the *Comedy*, an allusion to the *Inferno*, was made in 1313–1314 by the Tuscan poet Francesco da Barberino, in a commentary on one of his own love poems.

It was in the Verona years that Dante revised the *Inferno*, wrote and revised the *Purgatorio*, saw to the copying and diffusing of the two canticles, and made considerable headway on the *Paradiso*. This fabulous productivity resulted in part from his living conditions in Verona: a version in small of the tranquility and ideal rulership he had envisaged in the *De Monarchia*. He was, in all this time, the beautifully accommodated guest of Can Grande della Scala.

Can Grande, who had been a lad of fourteen when Dante had last seen him, was now twenty-four in 1315 and the imperial viceroy as well as the lord of Verona. He had shared both those positions with his brother

Alboino, until the latter's death in November 1311. It was not long before Dante, observing his host with warm admiration, came to honor the qualities he would have Cacciaguida extol in his *Paradiso*: a heroic disregard for money, a capacity for the most demanding work, a munificence so remarkable that even his enemies could not keep silent about it. Drawing on the name Cane (dog), Dante draws attention subtly to the Veronese at the very start of the *Inferno*, when Virgil predicts the appearance of a greyhound that will bring peace and harmony to Italy by routing the forces of disharmony, as represented by the leopard, the lion, and the she-wolf.

The man himself comes down to us as tall and strikingly handsome, soldierly in bearing, and normally gracious in manner, though he could also be quick-tempered and obstinate. Villani describes him as the richest and most powerful ruler of all time in Lombardy; and Boccaccio finds him second only to Frederick II in stately magnificence. These accolades testify, among other things, to Can Grande's masterful performance as viceroy, bringing Brescia back from Guelph control into the imperial fold (which Henry VII had never been able to do), rescuing Vicenza from the Paduan

Guelphs, and then making peace with Padua. Under the leadership of Can Grande, three cities in north-central Italy — Verona, Padua, and Vicenza — were formed into a potent imperial league.

But for Dante, it was not less Can Grande, the patron of the arts and the host without parallel, who was most to be revered. In his letter to Can Grande from Ravenna, Dante recalled that, on arriving in Verona, he beheld not only Can Grande's "splendor" but also "enjoyed your bounty." Like other special guests, Dante was given his own apartment in the Scaligeri palazzo. Its walls were decorated in Dante's honor with images of the Muses (for visiting soldiers there were portrayals of Victory; for preachers, symbols of Paradise). Elaborate meals were served him, with musicians and jugglers providing entertainment. On occasion, Dante was invited to dine at Can Grande's table, a signal mark of recognition. Such bounty, Dante told the lord vicar of Verona, had exceeded reports — which he, Dante, had thought to be exaggerated. In the poet's phrase, "I became your most humble servant and your friend."

The Scaligeri palace, a large, rugged, unostentatious affair, occupied much of what is now called Piazza dei Signori, presided over today by a statue of Dante (from 1865), standing tall, hand on chin, his head bent slightly toward the row of windows from which he had gazed out so often. The broad rapid Adige flows by only a few steps away; and a narrow lane leads to the Piazza delle Erbe, crowded with shopping stalls, much like the *mercato vecchio* near Dante's home in Florence. Dante could not but have been drawn to these and other urban elements (like the Arena), but for all his extravagant praise of Can Grande — as "the magnificent and victorious lord, Vicar General of the Holy Roman Empire" — he rarely alludes, in poetry or prose, to any aspect of the city itself.

He mentions the Adige (*Inferno* xii), but only a stretch of it some distance north, toward Trento. He had almost certainly watched the annual Lenten race, the winner of which earned the green cloth that Dante bestowed metaphorically upon Brunetto Latini. But he never, for example, speaks of the church and monastery of San Zeno, Verona's patron saint, with its Lombard decor and its porch covered with sculptures of scenes that surely intrigued Dante — among them, that of King Theodoric riding madly to the devil.

What he did do, with his unappeasable

relish for the colorful or discolored byways of Italian history, was to introduce the twelfth-century abbot of San Zeno, in *Purgatorio* xviii, and through him the current abbot, and a minor scandal in the della Scala family. Gherardo, who served in the monastery during the reign of Frederick Barbarossa and who died in 1187, appears on the fourth terrace of Purgatory, amid the slothful, and presents himself:

> "I was Abbot of Verona, under the rule
>   of the good Barbarossa, of whom
>   Milan
>   still talks with grief."

The abbot then alludes to "one who already has a foot in the grave," Alberto della Scala, who would die in 1301. This person, says the abbot, will have cause to mourn over San Zeno:

> "because his son, deformed in his whole
>   body
>   and worse in mind, and who was
>   born in shame
>   he has put there in place of the true
>   shepherd."

It is not inaccurate; Alberto made his illegitimate son Giuseppe, a cripple and perhaps mentally defective, the abbot of San Zeno, which he headed from 1291 to 1314.

Dante had undoubtedly met Giuseppe, and as Can Grande's youngest brother he may have warranted a certain respect. But the poetic memorial that Dante contrived for him was coldly contemptuous.

The *Purgatorio*, to repeat, was written in Verona, and was in circulation before Dante left the city and went on to Ravenna in 1319.

The canticle strikes a heartening note at once. "To course over better waters, the little boat of my wit now raises its sail": so the *Purgatorio* begins, as Dante prepares (he tells us) to sing "of that second realm (*quel secondo regno*) where the human spirit purges itself and becomes worthy to ascend to heaven."

There are torments and troubles enough in the purgatorial experience, but the tone from the outset is that of hope refreshed, something the poet himself may have been feeling in his safe and comfortable Verona lodgings. It is exactly the feeling expressed by Manfred, the Ghibelline loser in the battle of Benevento in 1266, whom Dante comes upon in the first moments of the new venture, in the region called the Ante-Purgatory. He is golden-haired and noble in features, but Dante notices that one of his eyebrows is cleft. Manfred explains that he was pierced by a sword at Benevento but, dying, repented of his sins. He had been excommunicated by the pope; yet even the papal curse does not condemn him forever or mean that "eternal love may not return, so long as hope retains any of its green." That final phrase, about hope keeping its greenness, was chosen by Robert Penn Warren as the epigraph for *All the King's Men*, a Dantean thought that runs like a theme through the novel.

The Ante-Purgatory, the setting for the first nine cantos of the canticle, is the temporary home of spirits awaiting their turn to ascend the mountain. But "temporary" is a relative term in the second realm. Manfred is required to wait for thirty times his natural life, or more than a thousand years. On the other hand, Dante is pleased and surprised, a little later, to meet his old friend, the Florentine musician Casella, among a horde of more than a hundred spirits, all of whom had died fairly recently and yet are already being transported by angelically guided boats to Mount Purgatory.

At Dante's request, to solace him for the arduous climb in store, Casella sings a canzone of Dante that he had formerly set to music, *"Amor che nella mente mia ragiona"* [Love, speaking fervently in my mind of my lady]. It is a fitting choice, since the canzone is about philosophy as the human wisdom that can guide the mind and the will toward divine wisdom: a précis of the Purgatorial ascent, which concludes with Beatrice, Divine Wisdom incarnate.

The souls in the Ante-Purgatory are largely late repentants, individuals who delayed submitting themselves to divine mercy through some defect of character or because of an unexpectedly violent death. Manfred is among the latter, as is Buonconte da Montefeltro, the Ghibelline leader at Campaldino, whose body was washed into the Arno. As Buonconte finishes talking, there appears quietly another spirit who addresses the poet in her childlike manner:

"Pray, when you return to the world
    and are rested from your long
    journey . . .
Remember me, who am la Pia.
    Siena made me, Maremma unmade
    me."

180

Son la Pia. In the original Tuscan, remarks the Italian philosopher Benedetto Croce, the young woman's words "are so delicate that they seem to be sighed rather than sung, and they accompany as with music the utterance of that poor and gentle name." Let us listen to them:

"Deh, quando tu sarai tornato al mondo,
e riposato de la lunga via . . .
ricorditi di me, che son la Pia;
Siena mi fé, disfecimi Maremma"

Pia Tolomei was married to a lordly Sienese, who imprisoned her in his castle in the Maremma, the melancholy coastal region south of Siena, and then murdered her, perhaps so that he could marry another. She is a classic case of the wife as victim. Edith Wharton, replying (in February 1909) to a young Englishman who had spoken derisively of women who complained about their marriage, named Pia Tolomei, along with Iseult, Francesca da Rimini, and Anna Karenina, as "women who were discontented with their husbands" and for good reason.

Farther on, the pilgrims observe a soul sitting alone with watchful eyes. He is Sordello, a poet from Mantua; he is overjoyed to find himself in the presence of the Mantuan Virgil. Sordello (he died sometime after 1269) had lived mostly in Provence, where he had written a much admired poem about a Provençal baron. The work accused the French leaders involved of gross cowardice, and, remembering this, Dante breaks out in invective against war-makers in Italy. (More literary lineage: in 1840, Robert Browning brought out a long narrative poem named for Sordello, complex but full of energy and dealing with the man and his war-torn times.) Sordello leads the pilgrims to a little dell, where late-repentant kings of France and England, formerly enemies, now lie pensively and sing in harmony.

There is an exchange with Nino Visconti, Dante's Pisan friend who had been betrayed by his uncle Ugolino. Then, spent by all he has seen and heard, Dante falls asleep. He is awakened to hear Virgil saying, "Have no fear. All is well . . . You have arrived at Purgatory." Following Virgil, Dante mounts three stone steps and kneels before the attendant angel, begging admission. The angel carves seven *P*s with a sword on Dante's brow for the *peccati mortali*, the seven deadly sins that will be successively purged during the long climb up the mountain. Then, with keys given him by their keeper, Saint Peter, the angel unlocks the gate and the pilgrims enter.

Drama and allegory alternate, the two modes fuse and modulate one another, in the course of that climb, which continues through the next seventeen cantos. The allegory reaches its climax in the Earthly Paradise, with the elaborate pageant representing divine revelation in all its sources (the books of the Old and the New Testaments and others). But meanwhile, as the pilgrims ascend the seven terraces there is enacted what in the present context is the central drama of the *Comedy*: the process of Dante's imaginative self-exploration, to an important degree his self-forging. In this regard, there is more manifestly a story in the *Purgatorio* than in the *Inferno*, which consists mainly and overwhelmingly of an unbroken descent into the lowest depths of human depravity.

On the first terrace of Purgatory, for example, where the sin of pride is being purged, Dante makes himself confront his own pride — as a poet. The pilgrims have edged their way upward from the foot of the mountain, along a cleft some eighteen feet wide, to the lowest terrace. Here formerly proud ones are bending their backs under heavy burdens of stone. One of these turns his head to look up at Dante, who recognizes him as Oderisi of Gubbio (he died in 1288), an illuminator of manuscripts and a miniaturist. It is Oderisi who sounds the theme of what might be called cultural pride, the belief of painters and poets in their lasting supremacy. Take Cimabue and Giotto, he says:

> *"Credette Cimabue ne la pittura,*
> > *tener lo campo, ed ora ha Giotto il grido,*
> *sì che la fama di colui è scura."*

[Cimabue thought to lead the field in painting,
> and now Giotto has the cry,
> and the fame of the other one is obscured.]

For all his political and literary activities, Dante had kept a proud eye on contemporary achievements in Florentine painting. He had known both the artists mentioned by Oderisi: Cimabue (c. 1250–1302) and Giotto (1266–1337). At age fifteen, Dante is thought to have joined the procession celebrating Cimabue's *Madonna*. He had become friendly with Giotto; and the painter, or perhaps an assistant, had painted a portrait of Dante, dreamy-eyed and sensitive, into the fresco of Paradise (now mostly faded) in the chapel of the Bargello.

Dante shifts the discussion to poetry, having Oderisi observe quirkily that one Guido has replaced another in popular esteem — Cavalcanti, that is, had replaced Guinizelli — but

> "perhaps there has been born
> one who will chase both of them
> from the nest."

Thus, anonymously, Dante again appoints himself the leading poet of his time. But he immediately undercuts this show of pride. "O empty flurry of human powers," Oderisi now exclaims (anticipating Andy Warhol's estimate of fame's time span), "how short a time does green endure upon the top." With audible sincerity, Dante, after listening thoughtfully to Oderisi's words, confesses that "Your true saying has filled my heart with holy humility, and lowered my swollen pride."

At Virgil's command, Dante stands up straight, but his thoughts are still "bowed down and shrunken," as he meditates on his presumptuousness. Engraved in the pavement of the terrace, he sees depictions of ancient pride, among them Lucifer, Nimrod, and "Troy in ashes and ruins." The confession of personal pride and the abject penitence have evidently sufficed, for there now appears an angel who brushes away the first letter *P* from the poet's brow. As they climb toward the second terrace, Dante finds the ascent appreciably lighter than the first. It reminds him of the path that wound up from the Arno to the old church of San Miniato, in its wild and wooded surroundings, one of Dante's favorite excursions.

But Dante the pilgrim is still somewhat uneasy about his former displays of vanity, even as Dante the poet may be uneasy about his manner of exalting himself through Oderisi. This is revealed in his remarks, on the second terrace, to one of the envious spirits. These have their eyes wired shut, so that they may no longer look with bitterness on the beauty or achievement of others; they are enveloped in fog and lean against one another, for comfort and to learn companionship. Dante is touched by the spectacle but reflects that envy had never been one of his worst faults of character. He conveys this to Sapia, a noble Sienese lady (she had been guilty of wicked joy at the defeat of the Sienese by the Florentines, but had later helped found a home for weary travelers). "My eyesight will be taken from me here," Dante tells her, "but only for a short time, for my offense is small." And then:

"Greater far is the fear by which my soul
  is suspended
      for the torment below, for even now
      the burden down there weighs me
      down."

Dante had called out to the envious to ask if any of them were Italian, and Sapia had answered from the crowd to say that here, in Purgatory, they were no longer divided by nation or state but belonged to the one true city. But perhaps Dante had meant, Are there any here who were once pilgrims or sojourners in Italy? The exchange lies behind the startling sequence in the next canto, xiv, where Dante, with the help of two spirits from Forlì and nearby, traces the course of the Arno River as a steady descent into savagery and hatred, making a pilgrim of any man of good will.

Guido del Duca and Rinieri da Calboli have been leaning against one another, listening to Dante and Sapia. One of them asks Dante where he comes from. And Dante:

"Through the midst of Tuscany
there spreads a stream which rises in
Falterona,
a course of one hundred miles does not
suffice it.
From its banks I bring this form."

"You are talking about the Arno," Guido comments; and Rinieri wonders why Dante had not named the river, as though it were something horrible. It is fitting, Guido tells him, that the river's name should perish, "for from its beginning . . . virtue is driven out as enemy by all." He then traces its malevolent course.

It begins in the Casentino — on Monte Falterona, as Dante had said — and first takes its direction among filthy hogs: *brutti porci;* thus does Dante characterize the dwellers in the Casentino, some of whom had given him their hospitality on his intermittent visits. "Then," Guido continues, "coming down, it finds snarling curs," the citizens of Arezzo, to which the Arno turns sharply southward. "On it goes in its descent," we hear, until it finds "dogs growing into wolves," the Florentines. The "accursed and ill-fated ditch" (*maladetta e sventurata fossa*), having descended through many more deep gorges,

> "finds the foxes, so full of fraud
> that they fear no guile that might trap
> them."

The fraudulent foxes are the Pisans, Ugolino and the likes of him.

It is an unrelenting diatribe, a wholesale indictment of Tuscany and its people, the exile's furious song. And though the Arno in fact shifts geographical direction dramatically — now south, now west, now due north, now west again — its course as rendered poetically (John D. Sinclair points this out) is an uninterrupted descent, as though into the depths of the Inferno.

The third terrace deals with rage, seen as blinding — the souls are enveloped in smoke — and as destructive. Dante has a sudden vision of

> people kindled with the fire of anger
> slaying a youth with stones, and ever
> crying
> loudly to each other: "Kill, kill!"

Hate crimes of this sort, as they might be called today, lead Dante to puzzle over the cause of such evils: whether they arise in the human soul, or are stirred by outside forces.

Marco Lombardo, a Venetian courtier, whom Dante questions on the matter, speaks to him out of the smoky mist. "You who are living," he says, "refer every cause up to the heavens, as if they swept everything onwards, of necessity." Yet men are given freedom of the will and a light by which they can distinguish good from evil. "Free will, if it be well nourished, will at length gain the victory." The lines foreshadow Cassius's wise saying to Brutus in *Julius Caesar*:

> Men at some time are masters of their
>   fate.
> The fault, dear Brutus, is not in our
>   stars,
> But in ourselves, that we are underlings.

There is no more pressing motif in the entire *Purgatorio*. Time and again Dante returns to the thesis that men choose to do good or evil; they are not predestined or the victims of faulty environment. They are given free will; and similarly, though humans cannot achieve redemption without divine guidance and help, they can take an active part in the process. But Marco Lombardo adds the inevitable Dantean principle that individuals cannot lead a truly good life unless they belong to a good society; and for this they need a system of laws and a ruler who can enact and enforce them.

Virgil carries the discussion forward as the pilgrims make their way up to the fourth terrace, and after an angel's wing has brushed away another *P* from Dante's forehead. Love, Virgil instructs his companion, is what motivates the human will. Love is the seed of every virtue and of every deed that deserves punishment. The lecture is timely, for the two of them have now reached the fourth terrace, one occupied by the slothful: people guilty in their earthly life of inadequate love (*lento amore*, in Virgil's phrase), love that is sluggish. The slothful, in large numbers, are forced to run headlong, without stopping, every so often shouting out the names of the great exemplars of significant haste: "Mary ran to the hill country" (after the Annunciation), "Caesar . . . thrust at Marseilles, and then raced to Spain . . . Hurry! Hurry!" Among those speeding by is the abbot of San Zeno in Verona, whom we took note of earlier.

Higher on the mountain, on the fifth terrace, the avaricious are seen, bound hand and foot and lying face down on the ground, motionless. With Virgil's help, as they climb from level to level, Dante is coming to perceive that sinners are subjected to two kinds

191

of purgation. Some reenact their earthly sinning, like the wrathful, who clamor about killing. With others, the punishment reverses the sin: the slothful run feverishly, the proud are made humble under burdens of stone. If the avaricious lie with their eyes glued to the earth, unable to gaze upward, it is because they behaved so in their lives (says one of them, Pope Adrian V), taking thought only for material things.

Encountering among the greedy (xx) Hugh Capet, who was the ruler of France from 987 to 996, the travelers are treated to a bitter-tongued survey of French monarchs, all of it expressive of Dante's distrust of the breed and ending with an identification of Philip the Fair as "the new Pilate," because of his assault upon Boniface at Anagni. There are references to other insatiable exemplars of avarice, like Midas, but suddenly the entire mountain trembles, as if in an earthquake, and a chorus of voices is heard singing "Glory to God in the highest."

When Dante's terror has subsided, he learns that the upheaval marked the end of some soul's purgatorial punishment and that soul's freedom to ascend to heaven. The whole mountain rings with praise. The individual released turns out to be Statius, the Roman poet who died in A.D. 96. He was the celebrated author of the *Thebaid*, a long epic poem about the warfare between the sons of Oedipus, Eteocles and Polynices, and the failed effort by Polynices to wrest the Theban throne from his brother. (The tragic aftermath of that event was dramatized by Sophocles in the *Antigone*.) Dante professed a high opinion of the *Thebaid*, though it is scarcely readable today. But in fact Statius in the *Purgatorio* is a mostly fictitious character, a necessary pivot in the poem's dramatic sequence and its historical pattern.

He is, to begin with, an ardent disciple of Virgil. Rehearsing his poetic career, Statius says, "The *Aeneid* was a mother to me, and a nurse for my poetry." At this, Virgil gives Dante a quick look that says, "Keep silent." But Dante cannot help smiling; and when Statius asks why, Dante, now with Virgil's permission, reveals the truth. Before them is "that very Virgil from whom you drew power to sing of men and gods." At this, Statius bends down to embrace his master's feet.

But Statius had been converted to Christianity in his late years, at least in Dante's inventive account, and this too he attributes to the influence of Virgil. "Through you I became a poet," Statius tells Virgil, "and through you a Christian." The latter reference is to Virgil's *Fourth Eclogue*, written in 40 B.C., in which, in flowing tropes, the poet predicts the return of a golden age and a newborn child who shall rule the world and bring it peace. Dante here bespeaks the long-established medieval belief that Virgil, under divine inspiration, had foreseen the coming of Christ and the age of Christianity.

Statius is thus the indispensable link in the guidance of Dante through the afterworld and in the historical and cultural process there being traced: between the pagan master Virgil and the Christian figure Beatrice. Statius performs his function as well by asking about the fate of other classical writers and personalities: Homer, Antigone, Catullus, Terence and others. Virgil reports that they, along with other classical personalities, are down with him in Limbo, "in the first circle of the dark prison."

Statius himself had been held in limbo for seven hundred years, if we accept his arithmetic. Following that, he had been on the fifth terrace of Mount Purgatory for "five hundred years and more," stretched face down on the earth for his sin of prodigality, the companion sin to avarice. At this stage in the poem's thematic structure, the classical world and the Christian world, in Dante's vision of them, were balanced together, as it were in converse.

There are now three travelers mounting upward from the fifth to the sixth terrace. As they issue out upon it, Dante spies a cluster of hollow-eyed souls with emaciated faces, all of them utterly famished. They are the gluttonous, whose punishment, like that of the slothful, reverses their sin. Dante hears a familiar voice and with difficulty identifies a face; it is his old Florentine friend Forese Donati. Forese confesses to having "followed appetite to excess" on earth, eating and drinking without stint; he is undergoing the punishment — he calls it "solace," for it prepares him for salvation — of utmost hunger and thirst.

Dante is astonished to find Forese on Mount Purgatory, and so far advanced in his atonement there, "less than five years" after his death, in 1296. Having just heard Statius's tale of a centuries-long wait for admission, Dante confides to Forese, "I rather thought to see you still down below," among the late repentants, "where time for time is paid." Forese explains that his special dispensation was due to his saintly wife Nella:

"by her flood of tears,
by her prayers devout and by sighs,
she has brought me from the borders
where they wait
and set me free from the other circles."

This account, while helping to clarify the time system of Purgatory, is also a distinctive moment in Dante's self-remaking. In one of the insulting sonnets exchanged in the *tenzone* with Donati in 1284, Dante had described Nella as coughing and sneezing pitifully the year round because of Forese's neglect:

not from wasted humors in her veins,
but from desertion in her lonely nest.

Now, in an act of self-purgation, Dante presents Nella not as a cough-ridden hag, but as a loving and devoted wife, saving her faithful husband from aeons of torment, through her prayers and tears.

At Dante's request, Forese offers news about his siblings. His sister Piccarda is in Paradise, where Dante will meet her. As to brother Corso, still alive in 1300, Forese correctly and pleasurably envisions his death before many years, falling from his rampant horse while trying to flee his enemies in Florence and dragged toward what Forese assumes is the Inferno, "the valley where sin is never cleansed." The three Donatis are thus symmetrically distributed, in the Dantean manner, among the three domains of souls after death.

Forese draws attention to other gluttonous shadows, one of them Martin V of Tours, who was pope from 1281 to 1285 and who died from eating too many eels plucked from Lake Bolsena and stewed in Vernaccia wine; his face is even more shriveled, Forese observes, than his fellow penitents. There is also Bonagiunta, a poet from Lucca recently dead, who murmurs to Dante about a woman, still young and unmarried, who will show hospitality to Dante when he goes to Lucca. The reference seems to be to Dante's stay in Lucca half a dozen years before the time of writing. Bonagiunta also, out of his poetic lore, brings into play again a main recurring motif in the *Comedy*, that of Dante as a lyric poet.

"Tell me," he begs, "if I am seeing the man who invented the new rhymes (*nove rime*) beginning with *'Donne ch' avete*

intelletto d'amore'?" Dante in reply invokes
the phrase *dolce stil nuovo* and defines himself as a lyric poet:

> "I am one who
> when love inspires me, takes note and
> goes
> setting it forth, in the manner love
> dictates."

The Italian tercet ends with the phrase *"Vo
significando"* — literally, "I go signifying."
The Tuscan idiom meets with the verbal,
"signifying," so dexterously employed in current American black literary commentary.
And there is an extra appeal in the use of *vo,*
for the first person singular, *vado,* of the verb
andare: "I go." The usage, *vo,* is still heard in
southern Tuscany.

The poetic motif is picked up again in
Canto xxvi, through the appearance of the
Bolognese poet Guido Guinizelli. The three
travelers, by this time, have reached the seventh, and topmost, terrace, with Statius dis-
coursing lengthily to Dante, as they ascend,
on the implantation of the human soul into
the human body and the separate life of the
soul after death. It is a necessary sermon,
bearing later upon the crucial question of the
resurrection of the body; but it is also prosily

scholastic, steeped in Aristotelianisms — an intellectual interlude before the return to poetic drama.

The seventh terrace is alive with flames, within which the lustful submit to purification by fire in requital for the burning passions that consumed them in life. Dante can hear contrasting sets of names being chanted: those of the Virgin Mary and Diana (the Latin goddess) as examples of chastity; those of "Sodom and Gomorrah" and "Pasiphae and her bull" as instances of uncontrolled lechery. (Pasiphae, wife of the ancient king of Crete, Minos, himself now assigning places in the underworld, was forced by angry Poseidon to become enamored of a bull and to beget an offspring, the Minotaur.)

Dante greets all these spirits reverentially, as "souls who are certain of having a state of peace," whenever it may be — again emphasizing the relative lightness of the sin in question and hence of his own erotic misdemeanor. There are clusters of bisexuals, along with the carnally "normal," and it is from one of these that the voice of Guido Guinizelli is heard. He has been invoking the name of Pasiphae and explains that "our sin was hermaphroditic" (*nostro peccato fu ermafrodito*) but because they had behaved like beasts, they are required to call out the name "of her who behaved like a beast with a beast." He then introduces himself: *"Son Guido Guinizelli e già mi purgo."*

The announcement springs out at us, as it did at Dante. In a canticle that offers a succession of ear-catching identifications, the most touching is that of Pia Tolomei, the most engaging that of Guido Guinizelli. Dante is enchanted to hear the poet "name himself the father of me and of others better than me." The meeting, as was said, gives Dante an opportunity to rehearse his poetic ancestry, in particular Guinizelli and Arnaut Daniel, the Provençal poet whom Guinizelli called the *"miglior fabbro"* ("greater maker" or "artificer" — the phrase T. S. Eliot used in dedicating *The Waste Land* to Ezra Pound). But if there is unwonted intensity in Dante's presentation of his Bolognese predecessor, it is because Guinizelli's career, public and private, was an uncanny foreshadowing of Dante's own.

The older man was born in Bologna in the 1230s of the well-regarded Principi family. As a young man, he consorted with other poets in the city, exchanging verses and refining his conception of the poetry of love and praise and the *"cor gentile."* Guido married an attractive young woman named

Beatrice, of the della Fratta family. In addition to his prolific writing, Guido took his turn on the public stage, serving in 1270 as *podestà* of Castelfranco, a town to the east of Bologna. But in 1274, the poet and his family were forced into exile, following the expulsion from Bologna of the Lambertazzis, the leaders of the Ghibelline party to which they belonged. Guinizelli apparently found shelter in Verona, under the protection of Alberto della Scala, the father of Can Grande. He died there around 1276.

The work of Dante that came out of this literary background was of course the *Vita Nuova*. It ended, we remember, with Dante's declaring that he will write no more of Beatrice for the time being, but that in some future period he hoped "to say of her what was never said of any other woman." He prays that then his soul might go to heaven and see there "the glory of Beatrice." The review of his poetic development in these late cantos of the *Purgatorio*, through xxvi, prepares effectively for the actual appearance of Beatrice four cantos following, in the Earthly Paradise.

To enter that celestial garden, the three travelers must pass through a wall of flames. Dante shrinks back in terror, beset by images of human bodies being burned alive. Virgil calms him, saying encouragingly that only this wall "stands between Beatrice and you." Beyond the flame is the final stairway to the top of the mount. The three stretch out to sleep, one on each step; when he is awakened, Dante follows Virgil and Statius to the summit. Here Virgil must say his farewell: "You have come to the place where I can see no further . . . No more expect my word or sign." Human wisdom can take Dante no further; everything else that Virgil represents — classical poetry, the classical and medieval humanistic tradition — can no longer direct him. Christian revelation and Divine Wisdom are now the imperative need.

"Without waiting more," Dante recalls, "I left the mountainside, crossing the plain with lingering step" and approached the Earthly Paradise. Virgil had assured him, at the moment of departure, that his moral nature was now "free, upright and whole." The long drama of Dante's moral self-discovery and judgment has apparently come to an end. All the more jolting is the moral denunciation in store for him in the garden.

The Earthly Paradise (*il paradiso terrestro*), the summit of Mount Purgatory and the anteregion to Paradise proper, is the scene of the final six cantos of the *Purgatorio*. As he enters, Dante observes a lady singing happily and gathering flowers. This is Matilda, the genius of the place, whose task it is to instruct Dante in celestial meteorology. The water from the nearby streams of Lethe and Eunoe, for example (streams that cleanse the memory), come not from rain but from a fountain supplied by the will of God. Matilda is dimly related to the great Contessa Matilda of Tuscany, ruler of her region for more than fifty years (she died in 1115) and the most politically active woman of her time. But the historical person disappears into the allegorical figure, one who sings so sweetly as she moves along the bank of the streams that Dante is enraptured.

Dante, and his poem, have indeed entered the domain of allegory, and he now sees a divine pageant coming toward him, a panorama of divine revelation, and it is pure allegory. But it is also gleamingly pictorial, in modern parlance it is cinematic, and Dante summons all his resources to describe it. Seven lights appear above, with rainbow streamers filling the sky; they represent the sevenfold gifts of the spirit, as described in the *Book of Revelation* — wisdom, understanding, counsel, might, knowledge, piety, and fear of the Lord.

Below the lights there tread four and twenty elders, walking two by two and crowned with flowers: the twenty-four books of the Old Testament (by Dante's count). Following them are four creatures, each with six wings, their plumes full of eyes. Dante forbears from portraying them. "Read Ezekiel, who depicts them as he saw them," Dante suggests to the reader, in an allusion to Ezekiel 1:4–14, with its prophetic vision of a chariot and four beasts. ". . . I spill no more rhymes . . . I cannot be lavish." (The creatures are a man, a lion, an ox, and an eagle, standing respectively for the four Evangelists, Matthew, Mark, Luke, and John.) Between the creatures, moving majestically, is a chariot drawn by a griffin; his double being represents the divine and the human nature of Christ. Three ladies come dancing in a round by the chariot's right wheel: the theological virtues of faith, hope, and charity. At the left wheel, four other ladies clad in purple "made a festival": the cardinal virtues of prudence, temperance, justice, and fortitude.

The pageant, in its entirety, is Dante's allegorical image of essential Christianity and of the Christian church as it should be. The chariot is the church, propelled by the two wheels of the active life and the contemplative life. As the chariot pauses, blessed spirits float above it, singing, and from its midst, within a cloud of flowers,

> olive-crowned over a white veil,
> > a lady appeared to me, clad with hue
> > of living flame under a green mantle.

It is Beatrice. The sight of her affects Dante as it did when first "it pierced me before I was out of my childhood." Dante turns to Virgil intending to say that his blood trembles and that "I recognize the traces of the ancient flame." This is itself a Virgilian quotation: Dido's confession to her sister after listening to Aeneas' tale of his wanderings. Only a moment before, angels had been heard chanting another line from the *Aeneid*: "O give me lilies in full hands" (Anchises' closing words to Aeneas in Book VI). Dante has contrived a final poetic tribute to Virgil, even as the Roman disappears; and Dante weeps for the loss of him.

The Beatrice who confronts Dante is the personification of Divine Wisdom, that transcendent understanding that can illuminate the human mind and lead it to God. As such, she will be Dante's guide and teacher on the journey up through the heavens. But she is also and emphatically Beatrice Portinari, formerly of Via del Corso in the *sestiere* of San Piero Maggiore in Florence. By way of demonstrating this, she now berates Dante unmercifully. While Dante's tears fall for the departed Virgil, Beatrice says, "Dante" — the sound of his name is like a clarion — "do not weep yet. You will have other things to weep for." As Dante stares at her, she tells him, "Look carefully, I am indeed Beatrice." Then in an icy tone, "How did you dare come close to the mount?" She is so stern in manner that the attendant spirits ask, "Lady, why do you shame him so?"

Beatrice replies with an indictment covering the time from Dante's pursuit of her in poetry to his erotic meanderings after her death. She invokes the Dante of the late 1280s:

> "This man was such in his new life po-
> tentially
>   that every good talent would have
>   come
>   to wonderful fulfillment."

But Dante squandered that gift. She, Beatrice, had sustained and inspired him for years, but after her death Dante went astray:

"As soon as I was on the threshold of my
   second age,
      and I had changed life, he forsook me,
      and gave himself to others."

After she had become pure spirit, she was
"less precious and pleasing to him":

"And he did turn his steps in a way not
   true,
      Pursuing false visions of the good . . ."

In vain she appeared to him in dreams; he
paid no attention. Beatrice, the partaker of
divinity, is for the moment also, in part, the
jealous young neighbor in the *sestiere*. She
reflects aloud that Dante would have been
eternally damned, had she not gone down in
person to the Inferno to beg Virgil to lead
the poor sinner through the darkness and up
the mountain. She turns to face Dante and
to ask, as though she still cannot quite believe it:

"What allurements or what advantage
      were displayed to you in the aspect of
         others,
      that you had to wander so?"

Dante, weeping, replies:

"Present things with their false pleasure,
    turned away my steps
    as soon as your face was hidden."

It is a perennial excuse: you were gone, they were here. Beatrice lectures him on the making of proper moral choices; but when Dante fails to look at her, she commands him sharply, "Lift up your beard! (*alza la barba!*) You will grieve the more by looking at me." Dante's confession that he "recognized the venom of her statement," and venomous it was, implies that he had behaved like a beardless schoolboy, and that it was time he grew up.

A wave of remorse sweeps over Dante, such that he falls senseless to the ground. It is an apt reminder of the moment in the *Inferno* when Dante had been overcome by the story of Francesca. That marked the beginning of his moral self-inquiry; here it reaches its end.

After Dante recovers consciousness, the narrative reverts to allegory, with two visions of the relation between church and state. In the first or ideal relation, the griffin draws the chariot, the church, reverentially to the tree of knowledge, which now represents the empire. Dante is made aware that Beatrice is seated alone on the earth, near the chariot, with only her seven hand-maidens around her. Again the heavenly figure, she informs Dante of his sacred mission to watch closely the next spectacle and, after his return to earth, to write what he has seen.

There appears a second visitation of animals, an eagle, a fox, and a dragon, variously attacking the chariot and representing successive assaults upon the church over the centuries. The chariot-church is thereby transformed into a beast with seven heads and ten horns, and a harlot now sits upon it. A giant approaches who first kisses the harlot and then drags her away. Such is the wordless drama of the church under Boniface VIII (the harlot) and the French king (the giant) who courts and then defiles it.

Beatrice in the interval has become "sighing and compassionate," with a beauty of eyes and visage that, Dante says, completely satisfied his "ten years' thirst" (*la decenne sete*); in the visionary year 1300, it has been ten years since Beatrice died. The two are now, to a degree, reunited.

Dante and Statius are made to drink from the stream Eunoe, which removes all memory of unhappiness and wrongdoing. Dante confides to the reader that he could sing at length of this "sweet draught," but "all the pages ordained for this second canticle are filled." He can say no more. The canticle ends with a chiming stress on his "renewal" and the same astral allusions that conclude the *Inferno*:

> I came back remade from the most holy
>> water,
>>> even as new plants renewed with new
>>>> leaves,
>>> pure and ready to mount to the stars.
>>> [. . . *puro e disposto a salire alle stelle.*]

eight

Ravenna, 1318–1321: The *Comedy* Is Finished

In the spring of 1315, when Dante was working on the *Purgatorio* in Verona, he received an unsettling communication from the Florentine authorities. A ferocious Tuscan warlord, Uguccione della Faggiola, having seized the town of Lucca and laid siege to the hilly region of San Miniato, above the Arno, was threatening immediate large-scale invasion of Florence. The desperate city rulers, as one way to increase their defensive strength, decided to recall the hordes of Ghibelline and White Guelph exiles scattered across the countryside. The outcasts were offered reentry and pardon, if they would pay a small sum on the huge fines leveled against them and if they would appear as abject penitents, with naked feet and a rope around their necks, in the baptistery of San Giovanni.

The invitation was issued around the middle of May and reached Dante a month later, passed on by several friends. To one of the latter (a monk or a priest, seemingly),

Dante wrote a reply, in which he scorned the terms of the pardon as "ridiculous and ill-advised." He denounced the required "self-abasement," refusing utterly "to allow himself to be presented at the altar as a prisoner." To do so would be to confess himself guilty; the faint trace of guilt-feeling detectable some years before had now altogether vanished. He was, he said, innocent of any crime against the state. "Is this the glorious recall whereby Dante Alighieri is summoned back to the fatherland after suffering almost fifteen years of exile?" If a dignified and worthy offer of return were proposed to him, he would accept "with no lingering feet." Otherwise, he would continue to live away from his native home.

The letter was passed from hand to hand in Florence, and had a reverberating effect there. With the *Inferno* and many cantos of the *Purgatorio* in circulation, Dante was becoming recognized as a great poet, some were saying the greatest poet in Italy; and in a cultural climate where poetic achievement was highly valued, his opinions and judgments were becoming influential. The official Florentine rancor grew proportionately the more intense.

In August 1315, Uguccione della Faggiola inflicted the most devastating defeat on the Florentine troops since the battle of Montaperti in 1260. Maneuvering Pisan and Lombard forces and German cavalry, he left two thousand Florentines dead and as many more wounded. The encounter took place at Montecatini, not more than thirty miles to the west of Florence. Uguccione now controlled most of western Tuscany, and Florence was in a state of near panic. But the expected attack was never launched; a political and military revolt flared up against Uguccione, and he fled to Verona, to ally himself with Can Grande. He was killed four years later in a skirmish with the Paduans.

The unrelenting Florentine rage expressed itself in mid-October, in an order condemning Dante to be executed and all his property confiscated. So much was repetitious of the previous decree of 1302; what was new was that the condemnation now included not only Dante but also his three sons; all were "to have their heads struck from their bodies."

Dante's children had led an inevitably precarious life since their father was sent into exile. Their inclusion in the new decree meant, among other things, that all three were at least fifteen years old, this being the age at which males became eligible for decapitation. Giovanni, the eldest, was in his late twenties in 1315. He had taken refuge in Lucca and may have been there when Dante made his stay. Beyond that, he disappears from view.

Pietro, his second son, was a young man of promise. He followed after his father in the poet's wanderings, coming to stay with him in Verona and living alongside him in Ravenna. After Dante's death nullified the sentence of execution, Pietro was able to return to Florence and look after the family's property.

But Verona remained the city of Pietro's heart. With the financial support of Can Grande, he studied law in Bologna and acquired a certificate in jurisprudence; he was also declared qualified (because of his "strong moral character," it was said) for ecclesiastical benefits. In Verona, to which he came back at the end of the 1320s, Pietro became known and admired as a judge and citizen.

Looking ahead over his noteworthy career: Pietro managed to recover the family holdings outside Florence, at Camerata and Pagnolle, and enjoyed the income from them (money he divided with Iacopo). In 1353, he acquired a villa and extensive land in Gargnano, near Verona and in the center of the Valpolicella district (already famous for its wines), amid the hills on the western side of the Adige. The property remained with direct descendants of Dante for two centuries, until around 1540, when the only legatee was the young woman Ginevra. In 1549 she married Count Serégo, with the agreement that the family resulting would be called Serégo Alighieri. The present Count Serégo Alighieri, Pieralivise, is a man of courtly and quietly distinguished bearing who manages the wine-producing territory and the residential quarters with skill and grace, and is quick to be of friendly service.

Pietro Alighieri had literary leanings. He tried his hand at poetry, without much success, but over the years he compiled a full-length commentary in Latin on his father's epic masterpiece, a work indispensable ever since to scholars of Dante and of medieval literature.

Iacopo, born around 1296, joined his father in Verona, if he did not actually accompany him there from Lucca and Tuscany. He too received benefits from Can Grande, who set him up with a comfortable income for literary study. Iacopo went on to Ravenna with his father and apparently stayed on there. He likewise worked intently over the *Comedy*, composing a carefully planned "design" of the *Inferno*, a tracing of its structure and sequences.

Then there was Antonia, Dante's only daughter, born at the turn of the century. She appears to have remained in Florence with her mother, Gemma, unmolested but threadbare until 1318, when the two women journeyed up to Ravenna to be reunited with husband and father. It was in Ravenna, in 1320 or the year following, that Antonia took the veil and became the nun called Sister (*Suor*) Beatrice, in honor of the name that Dante had celebrated in the *Vita Nuova* and was now poetically associating with the saints and angels in Paradise. Sister Beatrice entered the Ravenna convent of Santo Stefano degli Olivi. We hear mention of her as late as a document of 1371, where she is named as "Sister Beatrice, the daughter of Dante Alighieri."

Dante's decision to leave Verona, which occurred at some time in 1318, derived in part, one judges, from his incorrigible restlessness, but also seems to have derived from a growing aversion to certain aspects of life in Can Grande's palazzo. He was compelled at times to attend the court entertainments, to watch the buffoons perform their clumsy routines, to listen to the crude jokes that made the visiting soldiers roar with laughter.

In the spring of 1318, Dante received a letter from the lord of Ravenna, Guido Novello da Polenta, inviting him to come and stay; Dante accepted with alacrity. But he left Verona carrying with him a fund of admiration and affection for Can Grande della Scala, of whom he would prophesy great things in the *Paradiso* and to whom he would dedicate that canticle in a richly eulogistic letter.

The attractions of Ravenna were many and various. To the south lay the seaside town of Rimini, just below the point where the Rubicon flowed down into the sea, the stream that Julius Caesar decided to cross in 49 B.C. (as Dante knew). Here had lived the former Francesca da Polenta, who had married the lord of Rimini, Giovanni the Lame, and had been killed by him with her lover, Paolo. Francesca da Rimini was the aunt of Dante's new host, Guido da Polenta.

The city shone with traces of ancient history and former glory. It had been a Roman city since the second century B.C., but its period of grandeur really began in A.D. 402

when Honorius, for strategic reasons, made Ravenna the capital of the Roman Empire. His sister Galla Placida began the process of adorning the city with splendidly decorated churches, the feature for which Ravenna has long been most renowned. In 473, the Western Empire came to an end. The barbarian warrior Odoacre thereupon declared himself king of Italy, choosing Ravenna as his capital. But Theodoric, the king of the Ostrogoths — the eastern branch of the Teutonic tribe of Goths — promptly declared war on Odoacre, and after a three-year siege with thirty thousand men destroyed the enemy forces, and Odoacre, and took the title of king of Italy, settling in Ravenna.

Dante had been dimly aware of the Ostrogothic ruler as the one who quite unjustly imprisoned Boethius and ordered his execution; and he most likely had approved the sculptured scene on the portal of San Zeno in Verona, showing Theodoric being hurried toward hell on a stallion. Now he began to see other dimensions of the man. Theodoric, a little over forty when he became king, could neither read nor write; but he governed with intelligence and vigor for three decades, and with unflagging energy saw to the building and the decoration of several of the city's finest churches, along with a palazzo and a stately mausoleum, of hewn stone, for his own interment. Theodoric brought to the creations he supervised a deep feeling for the interplay of the Byzantine and the Western: as in the magnificent mosaics in the church of Sant' Apollinare Nuovo, among them a spectacle that must have stirred Dante to the core — twenty-six martyrs approaching Christ on his throne, followed by sixteen fathers of the church; a pageant magically akin to the procession Dante had portrayed in the Earthly Paradise.

There were personal pleasures in the city, as well. Guido da Polenta turned out to be a devoted adherent of the Florentine poet, and close and cordial relations were established from the start. Guido had come to power in Ravenna on the death of an uncle in 1316. A decade younger than Dante, Guido had taken part in a few minor skirmishes but was essentially a man of peace. In a modest way, he personified one of the major themes of the *De Monarchia*: he labored for peace as the sine qua non of a healthy life in literature and the arts. Several poems of his have survived, of no special merit; but he had been among the first to recognize Dante as *sommo poeta,* the "greatest poet" of his time. In the long perspective of history, Guido da Polenta is best known for his attentive hospitality to Dante Alighieri.

The hospitality included financial aid to the sons Pietro and Iacopo. With the exception of Giovanni, still perhaps in Lucca, Dante's entire family was now gathered about him: Pietro, Iacopo, Antonia (until she entered the convent), and Gemma. Dante, in his writings, is almost completely reticent about his family. He recites his own ancestry via Cacciaguida in the *Paradiso* and there are affectionate passing references to a sister and a brother in the *Vita Nuova*. At another extreme, there is the tale of Ugolino devouring his sons and grandsons. About the immediate Alighieri family, what indications we have (the commentary on the *Comedy*, the adopted name of Beatrice) suggest that the relations were amicable if also, as one suspects, distant.

In Ravenna, a literary and intellectual circle of sorts gathered around Dante. Its members included several Florentine exiles: Dino Perini, a poet of slight pretension for whom Dante had a genuine affection; the philosopher and physician Fiduccio de' Milotti; and the notary Pietro Giardini. Dante could talk with them in the Tuscan dialect about their old homeland and the possibilities of going back there some day. There is evidence that Dante did some teaching in the city, perhaps giving informal lectures on literature and theology.

Dante did give one formal lecture at this time, a discourse on the question whether water in its own sphere was in any part higher than the earth that emerges from it. He delivered the talk on January 20, 1320, in Verona, having returned there for this specific purpose. It was a dryly factual talk, enlivened only by a sardonic reference to the local clergy who refused to attend the lecture, fearing, rightly, that it would go against current church doctrine. Dante, armed with an array of astronomical and physical facts, which he had collected during his studies for the *Comedy*, argued unequivocally that water did not, anywhere, rise higher than the earth. The invitation to talk was itself a tribute to Dante's reputation as a scientific expert.

Dante's life in Ravenna, as he completed the final phases of the *Paradiso*, was further warmed by an exchange about Latin and vernacular poetry with a professor of literature in Bologna. He was known as Giovanni del Virgilio because of his devotion to the

Latin poet, and he had read the first two canticles of the *Comedy*. Around 1319, he sent Dante a Latin eclogue praising the Italian work but arguing that subjects of such grandeur could only be dealt with properly in Latin. He suggested some possible themes, citing in particular the smashing victory of Uguccione della Faggiola at Montecatini, and ended by inviting Dante to Bologna, where he would be crowned with the laurel.

Dante received the communication in high good humor and soon responded — it was a typical gesture — with a Latin eclogue of his own, exactly the same length as Giovanni's. In Dante's poem, the author appears as the shepherd Tityrus, his young friend Perini is Meliboeus, and Guido da Polenta is Iollas. Tityrus politely declines the invitation to Bologna, being determined to be crowned in Florence, if anywhere. To win Giovanni — who enters the scene as Mopsus — over to his opinion, Tityrus sends him ten measures of his best milk — presumably, ten cantos of the *Paradiso*. Giovanni, thoroughly delighted, replied with another eclogue. The answer Dante was able to compose reached Bologna only after his death.

The *Paradiso* had by this time been completed for nearly a year. He had made his journey through the heavens, guided by Beatrice, and had been bathed in the radiance of the Divine Light.

In the *Paradiso*, Dante ascends; he does not climb, as in the *Purgatorio*, but, as he is constantly remarking, is propelled upward with the speed of an arrow. He is swept up through the lower planets — the Moon, Mercury, Venus, the Sun; on through the higher planets — Mars, Jupiter, and Saturn; into the Fixed Stars; then upwards to the Primum Mobile, whence come all distinctions of space and time, of "where" and "when," though itself beyond space and time; to the Empyrean, the actual and eternal dwelling-place of the Three-in-One God, of the angels and the saints, of the community of the blessed.

The experience is a challenge beyond reckoning to the poet's resources of language and image-making; no one had ever attempted it before, as he tells us at the outset:

In that heaven which receives most of
    God's light
        have I been, and have seen things
        that no one,

descending from up there has the knowledge or power to retell.

Even so, whatever of that holy realm he was able to treasure in his memory "shall be the matter of my song." It is a statement of justifiable pride in his poetic self; and with it comes a warning — to those who have sought to follow him in their "little boats." "Go back to your own shores; don't commit yourself to the open sea."

Important truths about the nature and the locale of blessedness are disclosed to Dante almost at once, through his meeting with Piccarda Donati and afterward. The encounter takes place in the Moon. (Dante and Beatrice do not walk upon these planets; they enter them.) Piccarda is the younger sister of Dante's friend Forese Donati, and of the masterful and terrible Corso. She had taken the veil and was in the process of fulfilling her vows when Corso dragged her back into the world. He forced her to marry one Rosso della Tosa, with whom Corso was then seeking an alliance. (The two later fell out, and Corso went to his death trying to flee Rosso's henchmen.) Piccarda did not long survive the demands of worldly life. She had taken her place in

Paradise, along with Francesca da Rimini in the Inferno and Pia Tolomei in Purgatory, as the victim of a murderously bad marriage.

Dante is charmed by her but puzzled by her obvious contentment with her place in the lowest sphere of heaven. He asks her:

> But tell me, you whose blessedness is
> here,
>> do you not desire a higher place, and
>> to see more,
> and make more friends?

The question has a vibrantly contemporary — almost an American — ring. The word for "more," *più,* is repeated three times in the tercet: *più alto loco . . . più vedere . . . più farvi amici.* Dante assumes the natural Florentine desire to want more of everything. But Piccarda explains that the very essence of the blessed state is to be happy in whatever sphere of Paradise is assigned. Dante grasps the point and generalizes eloquently, "Then it was clear to me that everywhere in Heaven is Paradise." Piccarda Donati follows with the finest single line in the *Paradiso* (iii 85): "His will is our peace." It is a line that seizes the mind at once and repays long meditation: *"la sua voluntade è nostra pace."*

The meeting with Piccarda has raised another question for Dante, which he puts to Beatrice. If an individual's desire for good is strong, how can another person's wicked violence lead that individual to a lesser reward in heaven? Beatrice smiles, then answers that these spirits have revealed themselves here, not because this is "the sphere allotted to them," but as an indication of their degree of blessedness. All the blessed are in the final sphere, the Empyrean, but resting there they "feel more and less the eternal breath."

Beatrice concludes this phase of Dante's tutelage with a discourse on free will, "the greatest gift God made to his creation." The two are then flown effortlessly to the second realm, the planet Mercury, where Dante amid "a thousand splendors drawing near" identifies Justinian, the immensely active Byzantine emperor (from 527 to 565), whose lasting contribution to human welfare was his exhaustively devised legal code. It was Justinian's military commander Belisarius who wrested control of Italy from the Ostrogothic successors of Theodoric. Like Theodoric, Justinian beautified Ravenna with monuments and mosaics (like the stunning adornments of the Basilica of San Vitale); but Dante honored him even more for the just peace which he brought to the empire.

The whole of Canto vi is given to Justinian's learned survey of Roman history from Julius Caesar, down through Constantine the Great in the fourth century, to himself two centuries later, and Charlemagne two hundred years after that. Dante made a special note of Caesar's coming down from northern Italy to "issue forth from Ravenna and leap over the Rubicon," to initiate a civil war with Pompey.

The visiting lights sparkle and dance and sing, and then fade. Beatrice, after a pause, says to Dante, "Listen to me, for my words shall put before you a great doctrine." She proceeds to lecture Dante on the Incarnation: on Adam and the fall of man, on the long ages when "the world was sick down there," until it pleased God to send his son to live on earth and to atone for the sins of humanity through his crucifixion. The occasion for the theological lesson is not clear at first, but Dante's sequence is, as always, entirely cogent. We have simply moved from history — Justinian's talk — to the meaning of history. For Christian believers it was exactly the Incarnation that gave meaning to history.

The two travelers are now transported in

an instant to the planet Venus. "I had no sense of rising to enter it," Dante records, "but my lady gave me full faith that I was there." He sees glowing torches moving about in a circle and then, to his amazement, hears one of them chanting the opening line of his own canzone *"Voi che 'ntendendo il terzo ciel movete."* It is a proper greeting, for Dante has arrived at the *terzo ciel,* the third heaven. More than that, Venus is the last of the planets in Dante's heaven that is still shadowed by earth: that is, still populated by the spirits of those who in some manner had failed in their moral duty. Making part of this throng are those who failed because of erotic passion. Dante's poem, we recall, tells of being torn between his love for the lost Beatrice and his attraction to the "window-lady" (later and temporarily transformed into the type of philosophy). The spirit singing Dante's poem is Charles Martel (c. 1271–1295), a great warrior given to wantonness; and, as John D. Sinclair nicely puts it in the notes accompanying his prose translation of the *Comedy,* Martel is saying to Dante, "You are one of us." Dante accepts the designation, and the two engage in the exchange about the supreme value of being citizens that we have rehearsed above.

★ ★ ★

The ascent to the Sun is so swift and silent that it occurs before Dante is even aware of it. It serves him as a metaphor for Beatrice: it is Beatrice "who leads up from good to better with such suddenness that her action does not occupy time." He is now among the upper planetary spheres, and the demands on his poetic powers have become nearly intolerable. As the great master of language recognizes, it is the challenge to his word-summoning capacities. As to the Sun, "Though I should call up genius, art, tradition, never could I so express it as to make it imaged." Here, as in the higher realms, words volubly fail him. And he is doing what he says no human poet can do: he is evoking the very look and sound and texture of heaven.

In this ethereal setting, Dante provides one of his most vivid episodes. He recalls seeing a great many glowing lights moving toward him, alive and strong, circling and singing, and they were "sweeter in song than shining in appearance." And when these "singing, burning suns" had circled him three times, a voice comes from the midst: "I was of the flock that Dominic leads on the way." The speaker names a spirit on his right: "This was brother and master to me, Albert of Cologne. I am Thomas of Aquino."

Thomas, who was born around 1225 in Roccasecca, some sixty miles southeast of Rome, joined the Dominican order at eighteen and went on to study in Paris with the theologian Albertus Magnus. It was Albertus who introduced Thomas to the recently discovered moral, political, and metaphysical works of Aristotle. Thomas's philosophical and theological work, rooted in Aristotle, was unparalleled, culminating in the greatest work of theology in medieval culture, the *Summa theologica*. Thomas died in 1274.

"Thomas of Aquino" offered the most nourishing mind that Dante had met up with in his studies. For present purposes, what may be stressed — beyond countless particular considerations — was the appeal to Dante of Thomas's Christian humanism. There is a hint of this in Thomas's first words, an allusion to "the ray of grace whereat true love is kindled." In the work of salvation, Dante's ultimate subject in the *Comedy*, the Thomistic and Dantean outlook may be summarized in the formula "Grace does not destroy nature but perfects it." Grace enkindles, elevates, perfects. The opposite view, entering medieval culture from the powerfully appealing works of Saint Augustine, is that man can do nothing toward his own salvation; that, in effect, his human nature, with all its sinfulness, is wiped out and beatitude bestowed by divine grace. This view has been represented in our time, for example, by T. S. Eliot, counseling the individual, as in *Ash-Wednesday*, to remain motionless and let grace do its work: "Teach us to care and not to care,/ Teach us to sit still."

Aquinas, meanwhile, points to other theological spirits in his company, as Dante's vast learning comes again into play. Especially notable are the first-century thinker known as Dionysius the Areopagite, and Boethius, for whose unjust punishment Dante had a fellow feeling. Thomas the Dominican then delivers a stirring eulogy of the founder of the Franciscan order, Saint Francis of Assisi. It is cast in the form of an old-style romance, perhaps an early Dantean canzone, as Thomas tells of the affair in which young Francis was passionately caught up, with a lady "bereft of her first husband, despised and obscure for eleven hundred years" until Francis found her. Thomas then provides the key. "Francis and poverty are these two lovers." Preaching and the care and comfort of the poor are the features of the new order.

The stigmata received by Francis are then described:

> in that harsh rock between Tiber and
>   Arno,
> from Christ he received the final im-
>   print,
> which his limbs but two years carried.

The Italian has a kind of somber harshness, suitable to the subject:

> *nel crudo sasso intra Tevere e Arno*
> *da Cristo prese l'ultimo sigillo,*
> *che le sue membre due anni portarno.*

The event took place in 1224 at the rocky summit of a desolate mountain in the Casentino, in a hidden site reached by a plank between two boulders. Francis' hands and feet were pierced, like Christ's on the cross, and there was a wound in his side, similar to that given Christ by a spear. The saint died in 1226.

Following the spiritual biography of Francis, Thomas delivers a scathing rebuke to his fellow Dominicans for their uncontrollable lust for material things, in a dark contrast to the previous tale of the love of poverty. Now a second circle of lights approaches, singing sweetly and surrounding the first circle. It was a "great high festival dance," Dante writes, "of song and flashing lights, gladsome and benign." From among them, Saint Bonaventura, the Seraphic Doctor who became minister general of the Franciscan Order in 1257, gives a tribute to the founder of the Dominicans. Dominic (his life ran roughly from c. 1170 to 1221) was "a mighty teacher," Bonaventura declares, "a noble wrestler with the heresiarchs, a holy athlete." Dominic appears as a force rather than a clearly distinct human individual; the two eulogies, of Francis and Dominic, sound between them the paired themes so central for Dante — love and war.

Thomas talks knowingly for a spell about different church doctrines. Each member of the Trinity is hymned and exalted by the circling lights. Dante is then abruptly translated to the planet Mars, the very smile of which seems to Dante to have brought them up. Within the planet, Dante sees a cross formed by sparkling and moving lights, all chanting a hymn that thrills Dante though he cannot understand a word of it. The lights fall silent; one of them darts along the cross from the right side to the upright and down to the foot. It greets Dante with the words Anchises used to greet his son Aeneas in the underworld, "O blood of mine!"

It is Cacciaguida, the early twelfth-century warrior and crusader who initiated the clan into which Dante was born. He holds Dante's fascinated attention through Cantos xv, xvi, and xvii, with accounts of Dante's ancestry, of the sources of Florence's factional misery, and with colorful predictions about Dante's exile and tribulations after 1300.

Cacciaguida and his forebears were born where runners in the annual Florentine race cross into the last *sestiere*, San Piero Maggiore. The warrior speaks of his wife, who came from the Po Valley, "and from whom there comes your surname," Alighieri. Their son, Alighiero I, still roams the first terrace of Purgatory, where Dante has met him. "He is your grandfather's father." The Florence of those ancient days was a better place, populated by simple, pious, hardworking folk, only a fifth of its present size (perhaps sixteen thousand people). Cacciaguida names some of the old families that gave the city its great strength and simplicity — Catellini, Greci, Sacchetti, Giuochi, Caponsacco (the family of Beatrice's mother) — and he remarks that one of the gates through which one entered the city in the old wall-circuit was named for the extremely modest family of della Pera (it was near the amphitheater; a plaque at the corner of Borgo dei Greci and Piazza San Firenze identifies it). But family enmity and greed led to the "glorious just city" being dyed bloodred by division; and he recites the epitaph for Buondelmonte, slain on Easter morning in 1216:

> To that mutilated stone which guards
> the bridge
>> it was fitting that Florence should
>> give a victim
> in the last hour of peace.

Dante ventures to ask about his own future, having heard disturbing hints about it — "heavy words" is his phrase — from others. Cacciaguida replies that Dante will be driven from Florence; this is already being plotted by the pope. He will abandon everything. His fellow exiles will come to seem mad and impious until he makes himself a party of one. He will seek refuge with the lords of Verona, Bartolomeo della Scala and, later, Can Grande. Cacciaguida then issues his celestial instructions: "Make your vision manifest. Tell of what has been shown you in these wheels of Paradise, upon the mount, and in the dolorous valley." Complete your poem and circulate it.

Other saintly warriors are named, as their lights glimmer and skim along the cross. With Beatrice, whose smile seems to him more lustrous than ever, Dante is taken magically in a great sweeping arc up to the sixth sphere, the planet Jupiter. It is the abode of the just and merciful kings, and its motto is spelled out in successive letters by flickering lights. Dante finally puts it together: "Love righteousness, you who are the judges of the earth" (from the *Wisdom of Solomon*). After meditating on the thought for a time, Dante arrives at a bothersome question about just judgment.

What of the virtuous heathen? he asks. The query is addressed to a cluster of flickering lights taking the form of an eagle, a soaring emblem of justice. The eagle's beak makes answering sounds that "Never voice did convey, nor ink write, nor fantasy comprehend." He persists in his inquiry. A man is born in a place where there is no one to teach him about Christ, where no one can read or write. All his desires and his actions are good; he leads a sinless life but dies unbaptized. "Where is the justice that condemns him?" The eagle's beak, wheeling and singing, answers by telling the poet in effect to stop talking. "Who are you that would pass judgment on God, the source of all justice? No one who did not believe in Christ has ever risen to this realm."

The voice adds ominously that many who do profess to love Christ end in the depths of hell and adds what Sinclair calls a "royal black list," a catalogue of bad kings down through Philip the Fair of France. In the course of the listing, a covert Dantean judgment is conveyed to the reader. The initial letters of the nine stanzas three times spell out LUE: a medieval Italian word (*lue*) meaning plague or, more precisely, a contagious disease like syphilis. Sinclair remarks on this, adding that the letters mean that or they mean nothing, and "In Dante, nothing means nothing."

In the following canto, xx, the eagle softens, confiding to Dante that quite a few good pagans have been saved. He mentions, as an example, the Roman emperor Trajan (died A.D. 117), a warrior of large public concern and human appeal; he was admitted to heaven — Thomas Aquinas is the source of the legend — through the prayers for him, almost five centuries later, of Pope Gregory I.

The martial music gives way to an enveloping silence, symbolic, Dante comes to realize, of his new setting and its inhabitants. He is now in the "seventh splendor," as Beatrice calls it: the planet Saturn, the abode of the contemplative. A representative here is Saint Benedict, the sixth-century founder of the monastery at Monte Cassino. Dante becomes aware of a ladder "erected upward so high that my sight could not follow it." It is the ladder to heaven that Jacob dreamed of; Dante sees "splendors" ascending and descending it. Benedict and his followers are gathered up it "like a whirlwind," and Beatrice, with a brief gesture, has Dante "thrust" after him, on the ladder. "Never was motion so swift."

It is a brilliantly imaged moment. In the spiritual ascension, Dante has arrived beyond the planets at the realm of the Fixed Stars: beyond the vast groups of the individually redeemed — beyond the contemplatives, the lawgivers, and the warriors, the theologians and philosophers — and those, lower yet, who were tainted by the worldly passions or were tardy in their vows.

As Dante conceives it, he has in a sense risen up to his own. For he finds himself, in this astral domain, in the constellation of Gemini, under whose sign he was born. Within the zodiac, Gemini was believed to incite the literary and intellectual powers of its progeny; and Dante, a fervent astrologist, salutes the constellation as the "glorious star, from whom I draw all my genius, whatever it may be." Gemini was in the ascendant between May 18 and June 17, "when I first felt the air of Tuscany." It is a climactic passage in Dante's voyage of self-discovery, and it is our source for calculating his date of birth.

Beatrice bids him look down through the spheres they have mounted, to the earth, whose "vile semblance," viewed from this height, makes him smile. She next commands him: "Behold the hosts of the triumph of Christ." Her own countenance is aglow, "her eyes so full of gladness that I must needs pass it by, undescribed." Visible before them are "thousands of lamps, encircling the sun," the redeemed encircling Christ the Redeemer. The Divine Light, so powerful that Dante cannot endure it, is, as he knows, the blinding ray of wisdom that opened the way between heaven and earth. Beatrice, understandingly, has him turn his gaze upon her, "upon what I am"; for she is not only Divine Wisdom but also his beloved. Altogether, she *is* Paradise, and "figuring Paradise," Dante says, "the sacred poem must make a leap . . . It is no voyage for a little barque."

Dante is made to see the Virgin Mary, "the greatest flame," who "drew all my mind together." To her descends the Archangel Gabriel, who crowns Mary with a circle of torches; and she rises out of sight. It is a rhythmic ritual serving to prepare Dante for the ultimate vision. The sacred process continues with the arrival of a group of caroling lights, out of which there shoots a "blissful flame" that circles Beatrice three times, "wherefore," Dante confesses, "my pen leaps, and I write it not (*non lo scrivo*)." The flame is Saint Peter, Keeper of the Keys of Heaven, and his purpose is to test Dante's credentials for admission to the highest realms. He subjects Dante to a celestial oral examination, questioning him on the meaning of "faith." Dante answers by quoting Saint Paul: faith is the substance of things hoped for. Dante is quizzed about his own faith, and in reply he recites his version of the Christian creed, beginning "I believe in one God, sole and eternal," citing Moses, the Prophets, and the Psalms as sources of his belief, going on to the Trinity, and concluding

> "This is the spark
> which dilates into a living flame, and like
>   a star
> in heaven shineth in me."

Like a schoolmaster wholly pleased with a student's performance, Saint Peter embraces Dante, his light encircling him three times, singing words of blessing.

On a personal level, it has been a strenuous *self*-examination, Dante's investigation into what he truly and honestly believes. By means of it, he has arrived at a full articulation of his acceptance — and the terms of his acceptance — of central Christian doctrine. He is, as a result, a genuinely changed man, and this is palpable at the opening of Canto xxv in an address, as it were, to the awaiting world. Should it happen that the sacred poem on which he has spent so many difficult years might overcome the cruelty that bars him from Florence, then

> with a changed voice . . . shall I return,
>   and at the font of my baptism
>   shall I assume the laurel crown.

In ensuing moments, Saint Peter is joined by James and John, the three of them — we are told obscurely — representing the cardinal virtues of faith, hope, and love. Dante strains to see John's body as well as hear his voice, strains so hard that he is temporarily blinded. John admonishes him, "Why do you dazzle yourself to see what has no place here? My body is earth, in the earth, and will remain there until the eternal purpose is complete." Dante, one feels, was working his way toward a clear understanding of the question of the resurrection of the body. In *Paradiso* xiv, responding to a query about the use of the sense organs in heaven, Solomon had spoken of the "sainted flesh" being resumed and the human person being therefore more acceptable to God by being all complete. In Canto xxii, Dante had asked Saint Benedict if he might ever see him with "uncovered visage," in corporeal form. Benedict tells him in a kind voice that his desire will be fulfilled but only in the "last sphere, where all the rest have their fulfillment." Mary and Jesus, alone among those born on earth, have ascended to heaven with their bodies. In all of this, it is the poet and dramatist as much as the wondering Christian who speaks. The literary artist needs corporeal beings for his songs.

There is time for one more diatribe by

Saint Peter against the greedy popes in Rome, his evil successors, "ravenous wolves" — Beatrice even blushes at the violence of his language (there is political rage in heaven, Dante wants us to know, as well as on earth) — before Dante is scooped up to the last sphere. This is the Primum Mobile, the First Mover, the source of all space and all time, the starting point of the universe in Beatrice's phrase. Dante, turning, perceives a point of light so intense that his vision cannot contain it. A circle of lights engirds the great light, and that circle by another, till there are nine in all. Dante is in the presence of the light of God himself, surrounded by the nine angelic orders. This is the ultimate reality that Beatrice has led Dante upward to look upon. The divine truth, Dante says, "had been revealed by her who imparadises my mind"; the poet's inventive phrase is *che 'mparadisa la mia mente.* " He worships her as the truth of God and loves her more intensely than ever as Beatrice. Gazing at her, he sees the same "beautiful eyes with which love had made a noose to capture me" when he was nine years old.

In the Primum Mobile, Dante discovers, all *when* is now and all *where* is here. Human individuals arriving there, consequently, are

243

invested with the angelic power — it is one of the most attractive medieval doctrines, emphasized by the Angelic Doctor, Thomas Aquinas — of seeing everything at once. They also possess the angelic capacity for bilocation, of being in two places at once — in the planet Mars, for example, and in the Empyrean.

Dante and Beatrice have now entered the Empyrean, "the heaven of pure light," in Beatrice's words, "light intellectual full-charged with love." The beauty of Beatrice now transcends all bounds. Dante is more overcome by it than any poet, comic or tragic, ever could have been. But it is still the young woman on Via del Corso whom he acknowledges, even as he abandons the theme:

> From the first day in this life I saw her face,
>> until this sight, my song ceased not pursuing her.

But now his "tracking" must come to an end, "as at its utmost reach must that of every artist."

"The soldiery of Paradise" is what Dante looks upon in the Empyrean, the tenth and final realm: the redeemed of the earth in their eternal home. The military image prepares for the notice by Beatrice of the place being saved "for the lofty Henry" — Henry VII of Luxembourg — "who will come to set Italy straight, before she is ready for it." Dante, writing in 1320, knew that the late Henry's efforts had dwindled and failed; and he does not miss the occasion to denounce those who thwarted the efforts, Popes Clement V and Boniface VIII, who are envisioned as being thrust down to the lower depths of Hell.

The redeemed are arranged as the petals on a vast rose. Angels, like a swarm of bees, fly back and forth between them and God, bringing both utter peace and passionate love, Dante's two ideals of perfection. Seeing this, Dante reflects on the distances he has traveled, "from the human to the divine, from time to the eternal, from Florence to a people just and sane."

His last guide appears: Saint Bernard of Clairvaux, twelfth-century monk and mystic, founder of monasteries, special devotee of the Virgin Mary. He is a complete person, his eyes and cheeks filled with gladness, gesturing kindly. Bernard tells Dante that Beatrice is now in the "third from the highest rank, where her merit is assigned her." Dante offers a farewell prayer to her who had drawn him from slavery to power. Bernard urges Dante to raise his eyes to the remotest circle, where the poet sees more than a thousand angels glowing and dancing, and amid them, "smiling at their sport, and their songs, a beauty that was gladness in the eyes of all the other saints": the Virgin Mary.

In the concluding canto, Bernard beseeches the Virgin Mary to permit Dante to look upon God. Dante's sight is purged, and he looks into the ray of light that is the very light of Truth. The poet resorts to a necessary game with himself, now saying that it is impossible to describe the divine light — "my vision almost wholly fails me" — now challenging his memory to restore the vision, and begging God for help:

"Give my tongue such power
    That it may leave at least a single
        sparkle of your glory
    For people to come;
By returning a little to my memory
    somewhat,
        and with a little something in these
            verses,
        your victory will be complete.

So it is. With a scarcely controlled voice,

Dante can tell us that he united his glance "with the Infinite Worth."

> And within its depths, I saw ingathered,
>   bound by love in a single volume,
>   the scattered leaves of all the universe.

As his vision fades, Dante rejoices, in a last hymn of praise, that his own being is moved by the same love that moves all the planets he has mounted through.

> My desire and will
> like a wheel that spins with even motion
> were revolved by the love
> that moves the sun and the other stars.

The *Paradiso* closes with an invocation of the stars, as in the *Inferno* and *Purgatorio*:

l'amor che move il sole e l'altre stelle.

The *Paradiso* was completed at some time in 1320, and began to circulate immediately. In the time following, Dante enjoyed himself with his literary associates in Ravenna and in jaunty poetic exchanges with Giovanni del Virgilio in Bologna. Then, in the spring of 1321, he was called upon once more to perform a public service. Ships from Venice and Ravenna had, apparently, run into one another in the Adriatic waters, and the two groups of sailors had engaged in violent fighting. The furious doge of Venice, Giovanni Soranzo, connived with the lord of Forlì and other neighboring rulers in an attempt to bring Ravenna to her knees. Guido da Polenta hastily dispatched Dante and several other envoys up to the lagoon city to sue for peace.

The beguiling legend has come down to us that the Venetians were so in awe of Dante's powers of oratory that they refused to let him address the meetings. The story suggests the extraordinary reputation Dante had achieved, with the circulation not only of the *Comedy* but also of the *De Monarchia* and other political writings and letters. In any case, the mission was successful enough to ensure a follow-up delegation that settled peace terms in September.

Coming back to Ravenna, Dante decided to make part of the journey by land. His route carried him across the marshes, and here he contracted malaria, even as Guido Cavalcanti had done twenty years earlier in a western Italian marshland. Dante died in

Ravenna on the night of September 13–14, 1321, at age fifty-six.

His body, crowned with the laurel wreath, was brought to the church of San Francesco in Ravenna. Starting a century later, the Florentines — who now claimed Dante as their own *sommo poeta* — began a series of forays to seize the bones and bring them south. In 1519, an emissary showed up with authority from Pope Leo X to take charge of the remains and deliver them in Florence to Michelangelo, who was more than ready to construct a glorious tomb. But the crypt was empty; Franciscan monks had taken them away for safekeeping. They were secretly removed again by the Franciscans in 1677 and this time were not rediscovered until 1865, when construction workers, remaking an adjacent chapel, happened upon them by accident.

Dante now rests in San Francesco, in a dignified sepulchre created in 1485 by Pietro Lombardo and adorned with a bas-relief of the poet. The epitaph, written soon after his death, speaks of his wanderings and his songs, and of his exile from his "unloving mother," Florence. The sepulchre is enshrined in a small beautiful temple built in 1780 by Camillo Morigia.

★ ★ ★

John Ruskin would say of Dante that he was "the central man of all the world." In Dante, "the imaginative, moral and intellectual faculties" of man could be seen at their highest and in perfect accord with one another. Dante, Ruskin held, gave the finest expression ever recorded of the search for ultimate truth. The words (in *The Stones of Venice*, 1851–1853) are splendidly apt and worth long pondering. But by "the world," Ruskin had in mind primarily the Western world, in particular England and the European Continent. And it has become increasingly evident with the passage of years that Dante is *the* universal presence in literature around the globe, to a degree matched only by Shakespeare.

Testimony to this is the Museo Dantesco, situated in the Church of San Francesco in Ravenna and presided over by the learned, cosmopolitan, and hospitable Fra Enzo Fantini. The museum, within recent memory, has held conferences and readings from Dante in Russian, Turkish, Romanian (a big affair), Portuguese, Spanish, Chinese, and Japanese, as well as in English (Allen Mandelbaum reading from his translation of the *Inferno*) and Italian. It is evident from the attendant commentary and displays that these worldwide readers appreciated the interplay of Dante's faculties no less than Ruskin.

Dante, of course, has been everywhere in Italian culture. Witness Michelangelo, probably the most ardent Florentine since Dante himself, a man who was said to have most of the *Divine Comedy* in his head, and whose work over a lifetime — we need to think only of his *Last Judgment* (1541), the most muscular and harrowing of the many panoramic spectacles that have come out of the *Inferno* — is rife with Dantean images and echoes.

Dante, meanwhile, has been "the defining presence in Italian literature," writes Jonathan Galassi, "the first to move the language out of the shadows of its classical past." The remark occurs in the afterword to Galassi's exemplary translation of the *Collected Poems 1920–1954* of Eugenio Montale, the greatest Italian poet of the twentieth century and Nobel Prize laureate in 1975. Montale's entire career, Galassi observes, was a creative struggle with Dante. "The book against which Montale can be said to work in his middle years is the *Vita Nuova*," with Montale likewise piecing together discordant love poems into a kind of novel. In the climactic period of *La*

Bufera (The Storm), Montale's poetry, ever more allegorical, "is increasingly haunted by the *Commedia*."

The presence of Dante in English and American literature over the past two hundred years has been so ubiquitous and so energizing that we can do no more than list some of the chief writers who belong to his progeny. On Shelley, and for all Shelley's antipathy to Dante's doctrinal ideas, the influence of Dante was overwhelming. *Prometheus Unbound* (1820), the last act of which — with its invocation to "weave the mystic measure/of music, and dance, and shapes of light" — comes straight from the *Paradiso*. *The Triumph of Life* (1822) is a revisit to the *Inferno*, in brilliantly managed terza rima, with Rousseau performing as Virgil. Byron's *The Prophecy of Dante*, a product of his residence in Ravenna, depicts Dante in his own Ravenna days but as a far gloomier figure — "on the lone rock of desolate despair" — than the Florentine actually was. Browning's poem "Sordello" (1840), as we have said, relates with tantalizing ambiguity to the character Dante meets on Mount Purgatory. These writers and their contemporaries drew largely upon the *Divine Comedy*; Dante Gabriel Rossetti led the way back to the *Vita Nuova*, to Dante's canzones

252

and other lyrics, and to the love for Beatrice that inspired them. He brought his Victorian sweetness to the *dolce stil nuovo* poetry that he translated and collected in a volume eventually called *Dante and His Circle* (1874).

In America, Emerson in his journals (spring 1846) spoke of Dante as "the central man" even before Ruskin deployed the phrase; though for Emerson, Dante was one of several icons — along with Socrates, Shakespeare, Michelangelo, and Jesus — who variously comprised the archetypal persona whose features have "stamped themselves in fire on the heart." Longfellow came upon the *Divine Comedy*, in the original, in Rome in 1828, when he was twenty-one years old (he may have previously seen one of the first English translations, by Henry F. Cary, which had appeared in 1814). Several decades later, after lecturing on Dante at Harvard for a number of years, Longfellow set about translating the epic. Working at times with his literary friends James Russell Lowell and Charles Eliot Norton, Longfellow completed the task in 1867: a work, says Newton Arvin, Longfellow's judicious biographer (1965), that despite occasional flaws is "almost Elizabethan in the range and freshness" of its unrhymed blank verse. In 1882, Longfellow inaugurated the Dante Society, a select affair that met at the poet's house on Brattle Street in Cambridge, and of which Howells was a faithful if sometimes intimidated member.

Coming closer to our own time, we find Ezra Pound thoroughly versed in the whole of Dante, including the *De Vulgari Eloquentia*. His magnificently ragged epic *The Cantos*, written over fifty years, dealt with the material (so he said dryly, late in life) "that wasn't in the *Divina Commedia*," and is a gorgeous miscellany of borrowing and inversions of Dante's poem.

T. S. Eliot's mind and imagination were infested with Dante over a literary lifetime. In a talk at the Italian Society in London in July 1950, called "What Dante Means to Me" (he had previously published a long essay on Dante in 1929), Eliot reported that he had first come upon the *Divine Comedy* in a prose translation during his senior year at Harvard (where Dante was still held in reverence) in 1909, and that now, forty years later, he still regarded Dante's poetry "as the most persistent and deepest influence upon my own verse." He cited particular borrowings, aimed at arousing "in the reader's mind the memory of some Dante-esque scene, and thus establishing a rela-tionship between the medieval inferno and modern life": for example, in *The Waste Land*, "the vision of my city clerks trooping over London Bridge from the railway sta-tion to their offices evoked the reflection 'I had not thought death had undone so many,' " from Dante's image of "the trim-mers" early in the *Inferno*. And we recall Guido da Montefeltro's hissing speech, which served as the epigraph for "Prufrock": *"S'i' credesse . . ."*

He goes on to remind us that in "Little Gidding," the last of the *Four Quartets* in the 1940s, he had inserted a long passage, written in tercets and intended "to present to the mind of the reader a parallel by means of contrast, between the Inferno and the Purgatorio, which Dante visited, and a hal-lucinated scene after an air-raid." It is the passage beginning

> In the uncertain hour before the morning
>> Near the ending of interminable night
>> At the recurrent end of the unending

It is rooted in *Inferno* xv and the meeting be-tween Dante and Brunetto Latini, with phrases carried over ("baked aspect" and others), and a voice in both poems crying

out, "What, are *you* here?" It should be remarked, though, that T. S. Eliot, in his con-
genital reaction against the "cheerfulness,
optimism and hopefulness" of the Victorians
and the Romantics — the words are from the
earlier Dante essay — found a wholly admirable consciousness of evil as the prime
quality of the Florentine poet, in particular
sexuality as evil: a theme Eliot disconcert-
ingly located at the heart of the *Vita Nuova.*

And in America, we have Robert Penn
Warren, the most complete man of letters in
our time, using a phrase from the *Purgatorio*
as the epigraph for *All the King's Men;* orga-
nizing an earlier novel, *At Heaven's Gate,* on
the moral structure of the same canticle;
and, in his last novel, *A Place to Come To*
(1977), introducing a young southerner
who writes his doctoral dissertation on
Dante and goes on to become a renowned
Dante scholar. Warren and his daughter
Rosanna used to read the *Commedia* aloud
to each other, night after night in the family's summer home in Vermont; and when
Warren was ailing, Rosanna taped the entire
Inferno for her father to listen to.

Warren, more than any contemporary,
represents the persistence of Dante in the
literary mind. In "True Love," one of his
last poems (1985), Warren's poetic voice

recalls how, at a tender age, he first saw a neighborhood girl whose beauty stopped his heart. Two years later, when they met, she smiled at him and "named my name"; the effect was paralyzing. The girl has long since disappeared from view:

> But I know she is beautiful forever, and
> lives
> In a beautiful house, far away.
> She called my name once. I didn't even
> know she knew it.

Warren's love-smitten youth is a Kentucky country boy, speaking in a sort of elevated Kentucky idiom; after the girl first calls his name, he says, "I thought I would wake up dead." But the poem is unmistakably and delightfully a thirty-six-line version of the *Vita Nuova*, phrase by amorous phrase, from the early childhood encounter to the envisioned beatitude. Dante's presence, here and in many a later American poet, sparkles and sings and smiles like one of the spirits in Paradise.

bibliographical notes

Primary Sources
Texts and Translations in the Order of Composition

Dante's Lyric Poetry, edited by Kenelm Foster and Patrick Boyde (1967). Vol. I: Texts and Translation. Vol. II: Commentary (very complete).

Vita Nuova, Italian text with facing English translation; by Dino S. Cervigni and Edward Vasta (1995). A model edition, offering a superb translation of both poetry and prose, a topical index, a glossary of archaic terms, and appended discussions of the work's structure. Professor Cervigni (University of North Carolina at Chapel Hill) has also been generously helpful in other ways (see below).

De Vulgari Eloquentia, Latin text and Italian translation; with introduction and notes, by Vittorio Coletti (1991).

Il Convivio. Text with commentary, edited by Giovanni Busnelli and Giuseppe Vandelli, with introduction by Michele Barbi, two

258

volumes (1934). *Dante's Convivio*, English translation by William Walrond Jackson (1909).

De Monarchia. Edited by Pier Giorgio Ricci (1965).

La Divina Commedia. After discussing the problem with Dino Cervigni (see above), and after reviewing other English translations I had worked with over the years (Laurence Binyon, Dorothy Sayers, John Ciardi, Allen Mandelbaum), I decided to follow Professor Cervigni's advice and draw primarily on the Temple Classics edition. This edition, with the Italian text and the English translation facing each other, consists of: the *Inferno*, published in 1900 and drawing largely on a previous translation by John Carlyle (the brother of Thomas Carlyle), dating from 1867; the *Purgatorio*, translated by Thomas Okey, published in 1901; and the *Paradiso*, translated by Philip H. Wicksteed, published in 1899. Again following Professor Cervigni's advice, I occasionally modernized verb forms and choices.

I have had frequent recourse as well to the prose translation by John D. Sinclair (three volumes, 1980 edition). Sinclair's commentaries, canto by canto, are richly informed and acutely perceptive, and I have borrowed from them even more than the occasional acknowledgment may indicate. For pleasure and stimulus, I have also reread portions of Robert Pinsky's verse translation of the *Inferno* (1994) from time to time.

The Portable Dante. Edited with an introduction by Paolo Milano (1947). For my purposes, this volume is particularly useful in its inclusion of selected letters from Dante to "the infamous Florentines" and to Emperor Henry VII, among others.

Other Resources and Commentaries

William Anderson, *Dante the Maker* (1980). The best and most thorough biography in English.

Piero Bargellini, *Vita di Dante* (1964). A lively overview of Dante's life by Florence's leading citizen in the 1960s and one of its chief modern historians. Lionardo Bruni: see C. A. Dinsmore entry.

Eve Borsook, *The Companion Guide to Florence* (6th Edition, 1997). The indispensable guidebook, newly updated.

Dino Compagni, *Cronica* (1968 edition, with introduction and notes by Gino Luzzatto). A detailed account of Florentine history from about 1215 to 1315, by an observer who lived through much of it.

Charles Allen Dinsmore, *Aids to the Study of Dante* (1903). This fine volume (dedicated to Charles Eliot Norton, Harvard professor of fine arts and translator of Dante) contains studies of all of Dante's writings. It is especially valuable, for present purposes, for its inclusion of Boccaccio's life of Dante, a portrait of Dante by his contemporary and friend Giovanni Villani (from the *Cronica*), and the engaging short life of Dante by Lionardo Bruni (1389–1444).

Steve Ellis, *Dante and English Poetry: Shelley to T. S. Eliot* (1983). A well-informed and sensitive study of this rich, complex subject.

Francis Fergusson, *Dante's Drama of the Mind: A Modern Reading of the Purgatorio* (1953). *Dante* (1966). Studies in Dante by the most cultivated literary critic and historian of his generation. Fergusson's concept of the "histrionic sensibility" (see his masterwork, *The Idea of a Theater*) works to special effect with Dante.

A. Bartlett Giamatti, editor, *Dante in America: The First Two Centuries* (1983). Perceptive, often eloquent essays by commentators from Longfellow and Lowell to Allen Tate, Francis Fergusson, and Robert Fitzgerald, skillfully compiled by the former president of Yale.

Amerigo Parrini, *With Dante in Florence* (translated by C. Danyell Tassinari, undated [1930]). A captivating tour of the thirty-one plaques attached to buildings all across the "historic center" of Florence, each bearing an epigraph from *The Divine Comedy*. The text includes a translation and explanation of each epigraph and a sketch of the background.

Giorgio Petrocchi, *Vita di Dante* (1983). The currently standard biography, by the leading Dante scholar of the day. Among other admirable things, Petrocchi provides crucial detail on Dante's political life in the late 1290s and regularly reviews the opinions and conjectures of his main predecessors. No less valuable for this biographer is Petrocchi's wealth of information about Dante's family.

Enciclopedia Dantesca (six volumes, 2nd edition: 1984 rev.). A massive compilation, with entries on every conceivable Dantean subject, under the general editorship of Giorgio Petrocchi.

Ricardo J. Quinones, *Dante Alighieri* (Twayne's World Authors Series, 1979). Handsomely composed, short (212 pp.) literary biography, with emphasis upon the artistic development.

additional acknowledgments

I am much indebted to the National Humanities Center, in Research Triangle Park, North Carolina, and to its directors Robert Connors and Kent Mulliken, for inviting us down there for a two-month stay in the fall of 1998. The purpose of the visit was to begin work on the biography of Dante, and to this end I met regularly with a group of Fellows all of whom were engaged in biographical research. As on previous visits, I was helped enormously by Alan Tuttle and his library staff. I have never experienced a place more conducive to humanistic work.

William Coleman and Edvige Agostinelli, good neighbors in Florence and academic friends at home, directed me (among other things) to the Dantean studies of Giorgio Petrocchi. John Hollander, drawing on his immense knowledge of literary history, had suggestions about Dante and T. S. Eliot. Nigel Alderman found for me the volume by Steve Ellis (see above) about Dante and English poetry. Lisa Haarlander performed feats of invaluable assistance, from library research to word processing. In the late stages, Daniel Avery pitched in with his usual good-natured efficiency.

In Gargnano di Valpolicella, across the Adige River from Verona, Count Pieralivise Serégo Alighieri received us graciously, told of the history of this Alighieri estate from the time of its purchase in 1353 by Dante's son Pietro, showed us the carriages for the wedding in the 1550s of Dante's last direct descendant, and took us on a tour of the property. (Timothy Ryback and Susanna Fox of the Salzburg Seminar kindly apprised us of Count Serégo.) He also very kindly gave us a letter of introduction to the director of the Centro Dantesco in Ravenna, our next destination. The equally generous director, Padre Enzo Fantini, narrated for us the bizarre story of the vicissitudes of Dante's remains over five centuries, showing us the final tomb, leading us past displays of Dante reading-conferences in diverse languages, and procuring for us a complete taped reading of the *Divina Commedia*.

In Florence, we had a long and fascinating session with Padre Roberto Tassi, pastor of the Church of Santa Margherita ("Dante's church," as it has come to be called), and we are grateful to George and Nancy Madison for introducing us to him. Padre Tassi is extraordinarily well informed not only about Santa Margherita but also about the entire *sestiere* where Dante and Beatrice once lived, and he took us on an illuminating tour of it. In Casa Dante, nearby, we were able to study maps of medieval Florence and Tuscany and a layout of the battle of Campaldino in 1289. To the Gabinetto Vieusseux, and its brilliant codirector Maurizio Bossi, I am grateful for bibliographic advice and for putting in my hands the life of Dante by Piero Bargellini.

I was fortunate in having, as my editorial associates, James Atlas, general editor of Lipper/Viking Penguin, who commissioned the work and provided several lively and fruitful meetings; Carolyn Carlson, as intelligent and thoughtful a manuscript editor as you could hope for; and Adam Kirsch, who went through the text with an eagle eye and detected many places that needed correction.

Throughout the undertaking, Nancy Lewis was my cherished collaborator and companion.

To the Meiners, finally, to whom this book is dedicated, my gratitude is unending: to Fausto in particular, for locating and driving us out to Alighieri holdings in Pagnolle; to Francesca, for digging up crucial information about the old fortress of Caprona; and most of all to Rita, for companionship and guidance to our entire family for many a year.

The employees of Thorndike Press hope you have enjoyed this Large Print book. All our Large Print titles are designed for easy reading, and all our books are made to last. Other Thorndike Press Large Print books are available at your library, through selected bookstores, or directly from the publishers.

For more information about titles, please call:

(800) 223-1244
(800) 223-6121

To share your comments, please write:

Publisher
Thorndike Press
295 Kennedy Memorial Drive
Waterville, ME 04901